JN079948

なぞるだけで、自動書記チャネリングが始まる

宇宙写経

光の宇宙種族とつながり、7つの能力が覚醒する

Cosmic Sutra Tracing

この本の二人の著者より

みなさん、こんにちは。

「宇宙写経」なんて、初めて聞く言葉だと思いますが、

その「宇宙絵文字」を宇宙から"自動書記"でダウンロードさせていただいた牧季（まき）です。

2018年から、「人類底上げ計画」が始まりました。

地球がアセンション（次元上昇）するために、私たちに課せられたミッションは、

それぞれが宇宙から直接、情報をダウンロードして自ら覚醒していくというもの。

意識を上げ、地球とともに次元上昇していくのです。

宇宙にとって、地球がアセンションすることは、とても大切なこと。

地球がアセンションし、私たちが宇宙意識となることで、宇宙存在との共同創造が始まるのです。

宇宙意識になると、これまでの常識がまるで違ってきます。

概念や制限を外し、心も体も自由になる。

コントロールやジャッジがなく、喜び・感謝・愛のエネルギーにつつまれた光の世界となるのです。

覚醒していくあなたのストーリーがこの「宇宙写経」とともに始まります。

さぁ、鎧を脱いで、一気に覚醒していきましょう。

ミッション始動！

牧季

Hello everyone! My name is Maki.

You probably are hearing the word "Cosmic Sutra Tracing"

for the very first time, but I am the one who had the honor of downloading the "Cosmic symbols" from the Universe through "Automatic writing".

Since 2018, "Humanity's Consciousness ElevationProject" began. In order for the Earth to ascend, we have been given a mission for each of us to directly download information from the Universe and awaken ourselves.

We will raise our consciousness and ascend together with the Earth. Earth's ascension is very important for the Universe. When Earth ascends and we embody cosmic consciousness, co-creation with the cosmic beings will begin. When we embody cosmic consciousness, our conventional wisdom completely changes. Concepts and limitations will be removed, and the mind and body will be freed. Without control or judgment, the world will become a place of light, surrounded by the energy of joy, gratitude, and love.

Your story of awakening begins here with "Cosmic Sutra Tracing".

Now, let's take off our armor and awaken!

Mission Launch!

Maki

はじめまして。

牧季ちゃんが降ろしてくれた宇宙絵文字のチャネリング翻訳と、

宇宙種族やマスターたちからのメッセージ降ろしを担当させていただいた

Le Soleil＊Sunny（る それいゆ さにー）です。

まずは、数ある書物の中からこの本を手に取ってくださったあなたに、心からの感謝と祝福を送ります。

この本を開いて、今あなたは、どんな感覚を持たれましたか?

ワクワクしたり、懐かしく感じたり、これから広がる未知の世界への期待が

ムクムクと湧いてきたのではありませんか?

その不思議な感覚が芽生えたのには、こんな秘密があります。

この本は、遠い昔に宇宙の源から命を与えられ、

この世界に飛び出したあの時に、あなた自身があなたに送った光の招待状なのです。

あなたは、自分らしく制限のない、自由な世界で生きることを決めて今回生まれてきました。

この本は、あなたが記した魂の計画を思い出すための手引き書です。

ページをめくるたびに細胞は活性化し、本質の光の姿が現れます。

さて、前置きのお話はこれくらいにして、愛と光の扉へどうぞお入りください。

Le Soleil＊Sunny

Nice to meet you. I am Le Soleil＊Sunny.

I was in charge of channeling/translating the cosmic symbols downloaded by Maki-chan, as well as channeling messages from the cosmic races and masters.

First of all, I would like to send my sincere thanks and blessings to you for picking up this book out of all the many books available.

What kind of feeling did you have when you opened this book? Did you feel excitement, nostalgia, or a sense of anticipation for the unknown world that awaits you? There is a secret behind this mysterious feeling.

This book is an invitation of light sent to you from yourself a long time ago when the source of the Universe gave you life and you ventured into this world.

You were born with the decision to live in a free world, free of limitations, to be able to live as yourself. This book is a guide to help you remember your soul's plan that you have written. With each turn of the page, your cells will be activated, and the light of your essence will be revealed. Now, without further ado, please enter the door of love and light.

Le Soleil＊Sunny

この本でできるようになること

この『宇宙写経』は、一人ひとりの内奥に存在する本当の自分自身（内なる神）に出会い、これから到来する宇宙時代を"銀河人"として生きるための7つの力を覚醒させることを目的に、宇宙連合や宇宙種族との協働により作られたものです。写経することで、心・潜在意識からアプローチし、魂・超意識という深い層にまで働きかけて振動を起こしていくため、7つの力が覚醒する以外にも、たくさんの"できるようになること"があります。全部で22枚ある宇宙写経の絵文字を眺めるだけでも、すでにあなたの変容は始まっています。ページをめくるごとにあなたの神性が開き、卵が孵化するように、内側から本当のあなたが姿を現すことでしょう。

This "Cosmic Sutra Tracing" was created in cooperation with the Space Federation and cosmic races with the aim of awakening the seven powers that will enable each person to encounter his or her true inner self (inner God) and to live as a "galactic person" in the coming space age. By tracing the sutras, we approach from the mind and subconscious, and work on the deeper layers of the soul and superconscious by creating vibrations, so there are many more "things you are enabled to do" than just awakening the seven powers. Your transformation has already begun, even if you only look at the 22 symbols of the Cosmic Sutras. As you turn each page, your divinity will open, and like an egg hatching, your true self will emerge from within.

1

7つの力が覚醒する

Lesson 1〜7を実践することで、ハート／ライトボディ／ハイアーセルフ／魂のミッション／サイキック能力／ソウルパートナー／星のDNAが開花。7つは連動しているため、1つが開かれると他の6つも開きやすくなります。

7 Powers Awaken

Remember the Memories of the Stars

私たちが地球に転生してくる前にいた、故郷の星の記憶を思い出すことができます。

星の記憶を思い出す

2

Release Restrictions and Blocks

過去世からずっと刷り込まれてきた概念や信念体系、制限、封印、カルマ、囚われ、思い込みを解放していきます。お金に関するブロックも解除するので、受け取り上手になるでしょう。

3 制限やブロックを解放する

❶ By practicing Lessons 1 to 7, the heart/light body/higher self/soul mission/psychic ability/soul partner/stellar DNA blooms. The seven are interlocking, so when one is opened, the other six are easily opened.
❷ We can recall the memories of our home planet before we incarnated on Earth.
❸ You will release concepts, belief systems, limitations, seals, karma, traps and beliefs that have been imprinted on you from past lives. It also removes blocks related to money, so you will become better at receiving.
❹ By connecting with 16 kinds of related cosmic races and guides, you can gain tremendous love and feelings of security. You will know that the Universe

Escape from Loneliness and Be Surrounded by Love

16 種類のご縁のある宇宙種族やガイドとつながることで、絶大なる愛と安心感が得られます。宇宙から無条件に愛されていること、決して一人ではないことがわかり、孤独とは無縁になるでしょう。

4 孤独から脱却し 愛につつまれる

Channeling Ability Opens
チャネリング能力が開く

5

神々を含む宇宙種族と安心安全につながることができ、彼らとのチャネリングが自然に始まります。それを皮切りに、自分のガイド（守護存在）や宇宙ファミリーからのメッセージやサポートも受け取れるように。

2028 年以降、頻繁に行なわれるようになる「宇宙人コンタクト」は、テレパシーでの会話が基本。7 つの力やチャネリング能力を開くことは、宇宙人コンタクトで大変役に立ち、また、人間どうしやすべての動・植・鉱物とテレパシーで交流する時代への準備となります。

6 宇宙人コンタクトや
テレパシー会話の準備に

For Preparation of Alien Contact and Telepathic Conversation

この宇宙は多面で多次元であることを感覚で理解でき、ジャッジや支配、コントロールのない世界へと移行していきます。また、多次元に存在する自己の認識や統合が進み、分散していた力を集約して使えるようにもなります

7 Being Able to Integrate Multidimensional Selves
多次元自己を統合できる

光を引き寄せ 光の自分を具現化できる

8

宇宙写経は、宇宙銀河や地球と呼吸・リズムを合わせ、意識を中庸にしながら自身の光をクリアにしていきます。すると、必要な人・物・事を引き寄せ、なりたい自分を具現化できるようになるのです。

By Attracting Light, You Can Embody Your Light-Self

---

loves you unconditionally, and that you will never be alone.

❺ You can safely and securely connect with cosmic races, including the gods, and channeling with them will begin naturally. Starting with that, you can also receive messages and support from your guides (guardian beings) and cosmic families.

❻ From 2028 onwards "alien contact," which will become more frequent, will be based on telepathic conversation. Opening the seven powers and channeling abilities is very useful in alien contact and prepares us for an era of telepathic communication between humans and all animals, plants and minerals.

❼ You can sense that this Universe is multifaceted and multidimensional, and move into a world without judgment, domination, or control. In addition, the self-awareness and integration that exist in multiple dimensions will progress, and you will be able to concentrate and use the scattered powers.

❽ Cosmic Sutra will match your breath and rhythm with the cosmic galaxy and the Earth, and clear your own light while keeping your consciousness balanced. Then, you will be able to attract the people and things you need and embody the person you want to be.

Table of Contents

宇　宙　写　経

宇宙絵文字ってなに?

~宇宙の高次存在から自動書記で降ろされたもの~

　宇宙絵文字とは、高次の存在（ここでは16種類の宇宙種族）とつながり、体を通して降りてくる文字や絵のこと。高次の存在と波動や振動が共鳴することで、まるで他の人が書いているかのように、スラスラスラ～ッと勝手に手が動き出し、そのときに必要な図柄や文字のようなものが描かれてゆきます。つまり、「宇宙から降りてきた自動書記の絵や文字」のことです。

　この『宇宙写経』は、日頃から宇宙連合や宇宙種族、マスター、神々と交流している牧季が、16種族とつながり、体を通してダイレクトに送られてきた宇宙絵文字の塊を自動書記し、それぞれのテーマごとに一枚一枚の作品にして編んだものです。

　そこに描かれている内容は、ひと言でいえば宇宙の叡知ですが、16種族が伝えたい宇宙の情報、状況が何層にも圧縮されています。

　ひとつの絵文字にひとつの情報、ではありません。その内容は多面で多次元、見る人によって見える層が異なるため、同じ絵でも受け取る情報や理解の仕方が変わってきます。

　たとえば、数字に関する情報が降りてきたとき、ある人は小学校の算数レベルの情報を受け取り、また別の人は高校の数学レベルの情報を受け取り理解する、といった具合です。そこに、優劣や正解／不正解はありません。また、あなたの波動や意識の次元が上がってくることで、同じ絵や文字でも受け取る情報や解釈が変わっていきます。そしてそれらの情報の中には、宇宙の叡知だけではなく、たくさんのメッセージやギフトなども含まれているのです。

　宇宙絵文字は、見ているだけでも超意識を刺激し、使っていない脳を活性化するため、チャネリング能力が開花するアートといっても過言ではないでしょう。

What are Cosmic Symbols?

~What was downloaded through automatic writing from a higher existence in the Universe~

Cosmic symbols are letters and images that are downloaded through the body by connecting with high dimensional beings (here we mean the types of cosmic races). By resonating your vibrations with high dimensional beings, the hands suddenly start to move freely as though someone else is writing, and the necessary patterns and letters at that time are drawn. In other words, they are *images and letters of automatic writing which came down from the Universe*.

Maki interacts with the space federation, cosmic races, masters, and gods daily. She has connected with the 16 races and, through automatic writing of cosmic symbols chanelled directly through her body, has woven each theme into pieces of work in the Cosmic Sutra Tracing book.

In a nutshell, the contents depicted here are the wisdom of the Universe, but the information and circumstances of the Universe that the 16 races want to convey are compressed in many layers. It's not one piece of information per symbol. The content is multi-faceted and multi-dimensional, and because the visible layers differ depending on the viewer, the information received and the way of understanding changes, even for the same image.

For example, when information about numbers is downloaded, one person receives information at the level of elementary school arithmetic, while another person receives and understands the information at the level of high school mathematics, and so on. There is no superiority or inferiority, or right/wrong answers.

Also, as your vibration and level of consciousness rises, the information and interpretation you receive will change, even with the same images or letters. And within that information, not only the wisdom of the Universe but also many messages and gifts are included. Just looking at the cosmic symbols stimulates the superconscious and activates the part of the brain that is not being used, so it is no exaggeration to say that it is an art that brings out the channeling abilities.

宇宙写経ってなに?

~あなたも自動書記ができるようになる!~

写経とは、仏教において経典を書写すること。もともと学僧が経典を学んだり複製して、全国に広めるためのものでした。時代が下ると、写経をすることによって功徳が得られると考えられるようになり、先祖供養、祈願成就などを目的として、現在でも広く行なわれています。

現代では、300字程度の般若心経を書き写すことが多いようです。一文字一文字、見本を見ながら写したり、丁寧に上からなぞっていくことで、精神が安定する、集中力がつく、脳が活性化する、などの効果も期待できるといわれています。

一方、この本で行なう「宇宙写経」は、仏教的要素はなく、牧季が16種族とつながって体を通して描き降ろした宇宙絵文字をなぞっていくものです。なぞっていくうちに、手が勝手に動き出すような感覚になり、見本や下絵がなくともダイレクトに文字や絵が出るようになる、つまり、いつのまにか"自動書記ができる"ようにもなっていきます。この現象は急に始まる場合が多く、突然のことでびっくりするかもしれません。でも、安心してください。急にできるようになるというよりも、"思い出した"というほうが適切な答えになります。なぜなら、この地球のアセンション（次元上昇）を手伝うために転生してきた宇宙の魂=スターシードのあなたは、自動書記の能力をツールとして使うために備え持って生まれました。なので、きっかけさえあれば、いつでもその能力を使うことができるのです。

ここからが大切なポイントとなります。自動書記をすると

き、どの次元のどんな存在とつながって、何を描き降ろすのか? 自分はちゃんとしたところや高次元とつながっているだろうか?……そう思い、不安になる人もあるでしょう。霊的次元や宇宙には、いたずらやコントロールが目的で近づいてくる悪意ある存在がいるのも事実です。

その点も、心配いりません。宇宙写経は高次存在やマスター、神々、16種類の宇宙種族と共同で作り上げているので、他の低次存在とつながることはありません。宇宙写経をしていて自動書記が始まったら、そのときあなたは高次存在と完全につながっているので、安心安全に描き降ろしていただいてOKなのです。

宇宙写経をしていたり、自動書記が始まったりすると、どこか懐かしい感じがしたり、嬉しくなったり、理由なく涙があふれたり、魂がふるえたり、細胞が反応する場合がありますが、それらはすべて、癒し・浄化・変容・覚醒の一環です。また、つながった先からメッセージやビジョンを受け取ったときは、いまのあなたがステップアップするために大切な霊性進化の鍵となるので、メモして内観してみましょう。

もちろん、そのような経験には個人差があるので、他人と比べて嘆く必要はありません。あなたらしい方法とスピードであなた本来の個性が花開くのを、縁ある高次存在たちはいつも傍から見守り、常に応援してくれています。宇宙写経は、自力で覚醒していくのを最大限にサポートする、宇宙時代にマッチしたツールといえるでしょう。

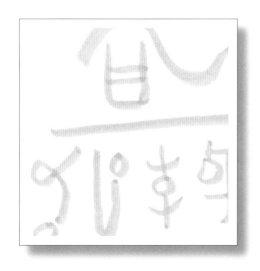

What is Cosmic Sutra Tracing?

~ You too will be able to do automatic writing! ~

"Shakyo" is the copying or tracing of scriptures in Buddhism. Originally, it was for scholar monks for studying and reproducing the sutras and spreading them throughout the country. As time went by, people began to think that copying sutras would bring merit, and it is still widely practiced today for the purpose of commemorating one's ancestors and fulfilling prayers.

In modern times, it seems that people often copy about 300 characters of the Heart Sutra. It is said that you can expect effects such as stabilizing the mind, increasing concentration, and activating the brain by copying each letter while looking at a sample or carefully tracing from above.

On the other hand, the "Cosmic Sutra Tracing" performed in this book has no Buddhist elements, but rather traces the cosmic symbols channeled through the body by Maki, connecting with the 16 races. As you trace, you will feel as if your hand starts to move on its own, and you will be able to write letters and draw images directly without a sample or sketch. In other words, you will also be able to do automatic writing. This phenomenon often starts abruptly and may startle you. But don't worry. A better perspective would be "You've just remembered" rather than suddenly being able to do it. This is because you, the cosmic soul = Starseed, who has been reincarnated to help the Earth ascend (dimensional rising), was born prepared to use the ability of automatic writing as a tool. So if you have a chance, you can use that ability at any time.

Here are the important points. When you do automatic writing, you may wonder about what kind of beings and in which dimension you are connected to, and what you are downloading. "Am I connected to a proper place or a higher dimension?"… Some may wonder and feel uneasy. It is also true that there are malevolent beings in the spiritual plane and Universe who approach us for the purpose of mischief and control.

There is no need to worry about this either. Because the Cosmic Sutra is created in collaboration with higher beings, masters, deities, and the sixteen cosmic races, there is no connecting with other lower beings. When you are doing the cosmic sutra tracing and when automatic writing begins, you are fully connected to the higher beings and can safely and securely draw as it's downloaded.

When you are doing cosmic sutra tracing and/or automatic writing begins, you may feel nostalgic, happy, or even tears may come up for no reason, and your soul may tremble or your cells may react. This is all part of healing, cleansing, transformation, and awakening. Also, when you receive a message or vision from where you are connected to, take note and reflect on it, as it is the key to spiritual progression, which is an important step for your advancement at this point.

Of course, each person's experience is unique, so there is no need to compare yourself to others and lament over it. The higher beings with whom you are connected are always watching over you and cheering you on as you blossom in your own unique way and at your own speed.

It can be said that the Cosmic Sutra Tracing is a tool for the cosmic age that will maximally support you in your own self-awakening.

この本の使い方

How to Use This Book

P21 から、それぞれのテーマごとに 7 つの Lesson が展開していきます。各 Lesson には、宇宙絵文字が 3 作品ずつ掲載され、徐々にステップアップできるように工夫されています。

From P 21 , 7 Lessons will unfold for each theme. Each lesson has 3 cosmic symbols, and is devised so that you can gradually step up.

各宇宙絵文字は、左ページにカラー見本、右ページにモノクロ図があり、見本を見ながらなぞり描きができるようになっています。カラーの筆ペンでなぞり、写経していきましょう。見本の色にこだわらなくても OK。好きな色を選び、自由に筆を動かしてみましょう。

Each cosmic symbol has a color sample on the left page and a monochrome image on the right page, so you can trace while looking at the sample. Let's trace and copy sutras with colored brush pens. You don't have to be particular about the color of the sample. Choose your favorite color and move the brush freely.

宇宙写経は、チャネリングしながら描いていくようなもの。それが自動書記につながっていくのです。自分のガイドと二人羽織りをするような感覚で、宇宙の力にゆだねながら、力を入れずにふんわりサラサラと描いていくのがコツです

Cosmic sutras are like drawing while channeling. This leads to automatic writing. The trick is to draw softly and smoothly without applying force, while entrusting yourself to the power of the Universe, as if you were sharing a coat with your own guide.

7 つの Lesson は、順番通りに行なう必要はありません。気になる Lesson からやっていくとよいでしょう。また、各 Lesson の 3 作品が終わる前に、他の Lesson が気になった場合も、そちらを優先して大丈夫です。

The seven lessons do not have to be done in order. It is a good idea to start with the lesson that interests you. Also, if you are interested in another lesson before the 3 works of each lesson are finished, it is okay to prioritize that.

なぞっているうちに、枠からはみ出てしまってもまったく気にしなくて大丈夫です。手が動くのに任せて余白に落書きしても OK。それが、自動書記につながる兆しであること、大アリなのです。"ちゃんとしなければ"を手放しましょう。

You don't have to worry about it at all even if it goes out of the frame while tracing. It's OK to let your hands move and scribble in the margins. That is a big possibility that it is a sign that leads to automatic writing. Let go of the idea of "having to do it right".

カラー見本の下に、Sunny がチャネリング＆リーディングした宇宙絵文字の解説が載っています。どんな存在のどんな意図によるどんな情報なのかを解読しています。写経をする前に読んで意味を味わいながらなぞってもよいし、写経をした後で読み、自ら感じたことと照らし合わせてもよいでしょう。正解はひとつだけではなく、あなたが感じたことがいちばんの正解です。自由に翻訳してみましょう。

Below the color sample, there is a commentary on cosmic symbols channeled and read by Sunny. It distinguishes the kind of information by what kind of intention and being it is. You can read them before you trace the sutras and trace them while enjoying the meaning, or you can read it after tracing and compare it with your own feelings. There is not only one correct answer, but what you feel is the best correct answer. Feel free to translate your way.

写経をしながら感じたことや思いついたこと、気になったことなどを書き留めておきましょう。あとで見返したとき、気づきにつながります。何となくそう思った、ふとそう感じた、ということが、高次からの大切なメッセージであることは少なくありません。

Write down what you felt, what you thought of, or what caught your interest while tracing the sutras. When you look back later, it will lead to your realization. It's not uncommon for important messages from a higher level to come up that way, with something you just thought of, or suddenly felt.

写経に使う道具
Tools Used for Sutra Tracing

宇宙との共同創造である宇宙写経に使う道具は、力を抜いて描けるカラーの筆ペンが最も適しています。なかでも、持ちやすくて書きやすい「あかしやカラー筆ペン彩」がおすすめです。何色かセットになったものを、ネットで購入できます。文具店や画材店では単品で販売しているところもあるので、好きな色だけ買うこともできますよ。

A colored brush pen that allows you to relax and draw is the most suitable tool for Cosmic Sutra Tracing, which is a co-creation with the Universe. Among them, we recommend the "Akashiya Color Fude Pen Sai", which is easy to hold and write with. You can buy a set of several colors online. Some stationery stores and art supply stores sell them individually, so you can buy just the colors you like.

「宇宙写経」に関わっている
16種の宇宙種族プロフィール

この宇宙には、私たち地球人のほかにも、たくさんの宇宙種族たちがそれぞれの星に住んでいます。とりわけ地球人に関係が深いのは、地球が属している太陽系や、太陽系が属している天の川銀河の存在。その多くは、地球人が創造されるときに自分たちの遺伝子（DNA）を提供し、その後もずっと、地球人や地球文明の進化・成長をサポートしてくれています。

「宇宙写経」は、そんな地球よりも少し高い次元から見守ってくれている、私たちの"先輩"に当たるたくさんの宇宙種族と、宇宙種族と同じようなレベルへと次元上昇した存在たちが数多く関わって生まれました。主要な存在は、ここに紹介する16種の存在です。

"宇宙写経をやろう!"と思った瞬間から、彼らは働きかけてくれていますが、ワークを進めるうちに、彼らとのつながりがさらに強く深くなり、より多くのサポートと恩恵を受け取れるようになるでしょう。その中には、あなたが地球に来る前にいた星の家族（スターファミリー）もいるはずです。彼らとの絆づくりは、近い将来、地球が"開星"して宇宙文明に参加するために、いまから準備しておくべきとても重要なこと。とりわけ、2028年以降には、彼らとのコンタクトが頻繁に行なわれるようになり、この16種族はそのメインのお相手でもあります。

この宇宙写経を行なうことは、その宇宙コンタクトに使われる「チャネリング」や「テレパシー交信」のトレーニングに、とても役立ちます。その取っ掛かりは、興味をもって彼らのことを知ることから。彼らはいったいどんな存在なのか、プロフィールを見てみましょう！

☆各種族のあとの（　）は、属する星座・星・領域を表しています。
☆→で示した名前は、その種族を代表するアセンデッドマスターです。

ET 種族
ET Races

リラ人（琴座）→エルモリヤ

七夕伝説の織姫で知られる、琴座に住むET種族。銀河系ヒューマノイドの原型種であるため、地球人と似た容姿。長身で長い首と小さな頭部が特徴。男女とも美形が多く、慈愛にあふれている。

Lyrans(Lyra) → El Morya

An ET race living in Lyra known as "Orihime" in the legend of "Tanabata". Because they are the prototype species of galactic humanoids, they resemble Earthlings. They are tall, have a long neck, and a small head. Both men and women are beautiful and full of affection.

アルクトゥルス人（牛飼い座）→サナトクマラ

6次元以上の高次元存在で、高い精神性と知識を有する。実体のない波動と意識の存在で、瞬間テレポーテーションをくり返し、時空や次元を超えて多次元に同時存在することができる。

Arcturians(the Cowherder)
→ Sanat Kumara

As higher dimensional beings beyond the 6th dimension, they have high spirituality and knowledge. As beings of insubstantial vibration and consciousness, it is possible for them to repeat instantaneous teleportation and exist in multiple dimensions simultaneously, transcending space, time and dimensions.

Profiles of the 16 Cosmic Races,

Involved in the "Cosmic Sutra Tracing"

In this Universe, in addition to us Earthlings, many other cosmic races live on their respective planets. Especially closely related to Earthlings are the beings of the solar system to which the Earth belongs and the Milky Way galaxy to which the solar system belongs. Many of them donated their genes (DNA) when Earthlings were created, and have continued to support the evolution and growth of Earthlings and Earth civilization ever since.

"Cosmic Sutra" was brought to life with the involvements of many cosmic races who are our "elders" who watch over us from a slightly higher dimension than the Earth, and many beings who have ascended to the same level as the cosmic races. The primary beings are the 16 races introduced here.

From the moment you had made your mind to do cosmic sutra tracing, they will have been working with you, but as you move forward in the work, your connection between them will become stronger and deeper, and you will be able to receive more support and blessings. Among them should be the star families from the stars where you existed before you came to Earth. Building ties with them is a very important preparation for our near future, in order for the Earth to "open" and participate in cosmic civilization. In particular, after 2028, contact with them will be frequent, and these 16 races will also be our main partners.

Doing this Cosmic Sutra Tracing is very useful for strengthening the "channeling" and "telepathic communication" used for such cosmic contact. The starting point is to get to know them with interest. Let's take a look at their profiles to see who they are.

☆ The ( ) after each race indicates the constellation, star, or region to which it belongs. The name indicated by ☆→ is the Ascended Master who represents that race.

シリウス人（おおいぬ座）
→ククリヒメ、セオリツヒメ

エジプトの神や日本の神として、地球の文明に影響を与えたET種族。クリスタルのエーテル体を使い、情報や知識をダウンロードしている。この種族をルーツに持つ持地球人にタイムトラベルの研究者が多数存在する。

Sirians (Canis Major) →
Kukuri-hime, Seoritsu-hime

An ET race that influenced Earth's civilization as Egyptian gods and Japanese gods. Using the etheric body of the crystals, they are downloading information and knowledge. There are many time travel researchers among Earthlings who have their roots in this race.

プレアデス人（おうし座）→空海

もとは金星の住人だが、科学とスピリチュアリティの進化と拡大を進めるために、現在はプレアデス星団（すばる）に移住している。人類創成に関わり、地球の発展にも多くの影響を与えた。

Pleiadians (Taurus) →
Kukai

Originally a resident of Venus, they have now relocated to the Pleiades star cluster in order to promote the evolution and expansion of science and spirituality. They were involved in the creation of mankind and have had many influences on the development of the Earth.

アルデバラン人（白鳥座）
→マーキュリー

ギリシャ神話の神々のモデルにもなったET種族。物質的な肉体は持たず、鳥類や馬などの動物、ヒューマノイドなど、相手と最も友好なコミュニケーションができる姿に変化する。

Aldebaranians（Cygnus）→ Mercury

An ET race that became a model for the gods of Greek mythology. They do not have physical bodies, and can transform into forms such as animals, like birds and horses, and humanoids, which allows for the most friendly communication with other beings.

ニビル人（ニビル星）→光のニビル人の父性意識

プレアデス星が、通信と人口密度の減少を目的として作った衛星「ニビル」に住むET種族。光沢のある青い肌と筋肉質な体格が特徴的。人類創生期に深く関わりを持つ。

Nibiruans（Nibiru）→ Paternal Consciousness of the Nibiruans of Light

An ET race living in the satellite "Nibiru" created by the Pleiades star for the purpose of telecommunication and to reduce population density. They are characterized by their shiny blue skin and muscular physiques. They are deeply involved in the creation period of mankind.

クラリオン人（太陽系12惑星）
→ヒラリオン

太陽を挟み、地球と真反対に位置するクラリオン星に住むET種族。クラリオンの1時間は地球の100年に相当し、光の速度で瞬間移動ができる。上空にオーロラが降りるとき、彼らの出現が多く見られる。

Clarions（the 12th planet in the solar system）→ El Morya

An ET race that lives on Planet Clarion, which is located on the opposite side of the Earth from the Sun. One hour on Clarion is equivalent to 100 years on Earth, and it can teleport at the speed of light. They are often seen when the aurora borealis appears in the sky.

金星人（太陽系）
→セントジャーメイン

慈愛と美的感覚に優れたET種族。発光体のボディを持ち、2m以上の高身長で大変美しい。古くから地球人にテレパシーでコンタクトをとり、多くの芸術家にインスピレーションを与えている。

Venusians（the solar system）→ Saint Germain

An ET race with an excellent sense of compassion and aesthetics. They have luminous bodies and are very beautiful with a height of over 2m (roughly 6.5feet). Since ancient times, they have been in telepathic contact with Earthlings and have inspired many artists.

太陽人（太陽系）→アマテラス

日本の八百万の神アマテラスと深い関わりを持つ、太陽に住むET種族。黒髪と漆黒の瞳、真っ白な肌が特徴的な容姿。エネルギッシュで大らかな性質。日本の皇室との関わりが深い。

Solarians（the solar system）→ Amaterasu

An ET race that lives in the sun and has a deep connection with Amaterasu, one of the Japanese multitudinous gods. Black hair, jet-black eyes, and pure white skin are the characteristics of their appearance. Has an energetic and generous nature. They have deep connections with the Japanese imperial family.

海王星人（太陽系）→マーリン

太陽系の海王星に住み、光沢のあるブルーグリーンの肌と半人半魚の容姿を持つET種族。水陸に適応性があり、瞬時に波動を変えて水中と陸に適した肉体に変貌する。伝説の河童のモデル。

Neptunians（the solar system）→ Merlin

An ET race with lustrous blue-green skin and a half-human half-fish appearance that lives on the planet Neptune in the solar system. Adaptable to both water and land, they can instantly change their vibration and transform into a body suitable for both water and land. Model of the legendary kappa.

☆このほかにも、風の時代のマスターであるニギハヤヒ、サナンダ、レディナダも、この宇宙写経に関わっています。

アヌンナキ種族（ニビル人）→イナンナ

惑星「ニビル」から金の採掘のために地球に飛来した。人類創生期やシュメール文化にも深く関与している。地球人への愛着が強く、地球の文明の基礎も担った、人類と最も関わりの深いET種族。

Anunnaki race（Nibiruans）→ Inanna

They came to Earth from the planet "Nibiru" to mine for gold. They are also deeply involved in the early human period and Sumerian culture. An ET race that has the deepest relationship with humankind, having a strong attachment to Earthlings and being the foundation of Earth's civilization.

龍族（シリウス星系）→宝龍

約2万5000年前の日本の青森に飛来し、地獣人の霊格向上のために日本人にDNA提供したET種族。この誇り高い龍族の血脈が、強い意志と調和を愛する日本人の特質に影響している。

The Dragon race（Sirius star system）→ Treasure Dragon

An ET species that came flying to Aomori, Japan about 25,000 years ago, and provided DNA to the Japanese to improve the spiritual quality of the Earthlings. This proud dragon bloodline influences the strong-willed and harmony-loving traits of the Japanese.

レムリアの民（地球内部）テロスの住人→アダマ

1万3000年前、レムリア大陸が太平洋に沈んだときに地球内部に潜り、「テロス」という地下都市を築いたレムリアの子孫。肉体を物質や気体、液体と変化させ、特殊な環境化に順応している。

People of Lemuria (Inner Earth) Inhabitants of Telos → Adama

They are descendants of Lemuria, who dived into the Earth's interior and built an underground city called "Telos" 13,000 years ago, when the Lemurian continent sank into the Pacific Ocean. They adapt to special environments by transforming their bodies into substances, gases, and liquids.

エジプト神族（シリウス星系）→イシス、セラピスベイ

シリウス星出身のET種族。古代エジプトの民に天文学や医学等の叡智を与え、神として崇められていた。壁画や遺跡に残る異形な姿は、この種族を模したもの。光と闇の番人。

Egyptian deities (Sirius star system) → Isis, Serapis Bey

An ET race from the planet Sirius. They were worshiped as gods and gave wisdom such as astronomy and medicine to the people of ancient Egypt. The strange figures that remain in murals and ruins are modeled from this race. They are the guardians of light and darkness.

日本の神族（グレードセントラルサン、シリウス星系）→アマテラス、アメノウズメ

天照大神に代表される日本の八百万の神々。太陽系出身ETやシリウスET等多数の種族が存在する。調和と共存意識が高く、大らかな気質を持つ。大和魂の基礎となっている。

Japanese deities(the Great Central Sun, Sirius star system) → Amaterasu, Ame-no-uzume

Multitudinous gods of Japan are represented by Amaterasu Omikami. Among them there are many races such as ETs from the solar system and Sirius. They have a high sense of harmony and coexistence, and have a generous temperament. They are the basis of the "Yamato spirit" of the Japanese.

ガイアの精霊（地球）→ガイアと名もなき精霊

女性性エネルギーを持つ地球（ガイア）のメッセンジャーの役割をし、地球人と共生している。自然界のあらゆるものに宿り、擬人化した姿の妖精や意識やエネルギー体の精霊が存在する。

Spirits of Gaia (Earth) → Gaia and Nameless Spirits

They act as messengers of the Earth (Gaia) which holds feminine energy and coexist with Earthlings. There are anthropomorphic fairies, spirits of consciousness and energy bodies that dwell within everything in the natural world.

☆ Other masters of the age of the wind, such as Nigihayahi, Sananda, El Morya and Lady Nada, are also involved in this Cosmic Sutra Tracing.

宇宙絵文字（写経）の読み解き

この本で紹介しているすべての宇宙絵文字には、16種族の宇宙存在やマスターたちのエネルギーが転写されています。なぞるだけでつながりが強化され、自らの波動が引き上がり、覚醒や能力開花が促されていく大きな理由は、高次存在たちのエネルギーに直接触れることができるからなのです。
作品のテーマに合わせ、その能力を引き出す力に長けた存在たちがあまた関わっています。ここでは、Lesson 1「ハートの覚醒」の作品をサンプルに、どんな存在が関わっているのか、見てみましょう。

転写されているもの
What is Transcribed

①リラ人（琴座）	⑨太陽人（太陽系）	⑯ガイアの精霊（地球）
②アルクトゥルス人（牛飼い座）	⑩海王星人（太陽系）	
③シリウス人（おおいぬ座）	⑪アヌンナキ種族（ニビル人）	
④プレアデス人（おうし座）	⑫龍族（シリウス星系）	A ヒラリオン
⑤アルデバラン人（白鳥座）	⑬レムリアの民（地球内部）テロスの住人	B ヒラリオンの贈り物
⑥ニビル人（ニビル星）	⑭エジプト神族（シリウス星系）	C ガイアの子宮
⑦クラリオン人（太陽系12惑星）	⑮日本の神族（グレードセントラルサン、シリウス星系）	D 地球人
⑧金星人（太陽系）		E アセンションの上昇気流

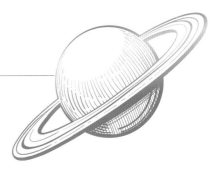

Interpreting the Cosmic Symbols (Sutra tracing)

All the cosmic symbols introduced in this book are transcribed with the energies of the 16 races of cosmic beings and masters. The main reason why tracing is able to strengthen the connection, raise one's own vibrations, and promote the awakening and flowering of abilities is that it allows direct contact with the energies of higher beings.

There are a number of entities involved who are skilled in bringing out the best in your abilities in accordance with the theme of each work.

Let's look at an example of the work from Lesson 1, "Awakening of the Heart," and see what kind of beings are involved.

●描かれているもの：銀河人の生誕祭
●テーマ：自分を受け入れる
●ヒラリオンからの贈り物：「光の翼」「どこまでも見わたすことのできる光の目」「すべての存在とコミュニケーションをとるための光の耳と口」「無限のイマジネーション」「老いや病とは無縁のライトボディ」

【解説】
　この写経は、私たち地球人が、尊厳高く美しい存在である自分を受け入れ、ガイアや自分自身に深い感謝と愛を向けることにより、まったく新しい銀河人として生まれ変わる生誕祭、その儀式の様子が描かれています。
　写経中央に横向きに映るガイアは、その体内に新人類を宿し、１６種族に見守られながら、いままさに新しい人類を産み落とそうとしています。
その誕生を祝うように、Lesson 1 のファシリテーターを務めるクラリオン星人のヒラリオンが、ガイアに光の贈り物をしています。その贈り物は、新生地球を生きるために必要な「光の翼」「どこまでも見わたすことのできる光の目」「すべての存在とコミュニケーションをとるための光の耳と口」「無限のイマジネーション」「老いや病とは無縁のライトボディ」です。
　この記念すべき誕生に翳りが混じるとするならば、それは古い地球で習慣化された反応（不安や猜疑心、自己否定などの分離意識）に過ぎません。それらに執着することなく、怖れを手放し、生まれ変わった奇跡を喜びのもと体験しましょう。

● What is depicted：Birth ceremony of the galactic people
● Theme: Accepting yourself
● Gifts from Hilarion："Wings of Light", "Eyes of light that can see everything", "Ears and mouths of light to communicate with all beings", "Infinite imagination" and "A light body, free from old age and disease"

【Interpretation】
This sutra tracing depicts the birth ceremony where we Earthlings accept ourselves as dignified and beautiful beings, and by expressing deep gratitude and love toward Gaia and ourselves, we are reborn as a whole new galactic people.
Gaia, reflected horizontally in the center of the traced sutra, is carrying a new human race, and being watched over by the 16 races, is about to give birth.
As if celebrating its birth, Hilarion, the Clarion who is the facilitator of Lesson 1, is giving the gift of light to Gaia.
These gifts are the "Wings of Light", "Eyes of light that can see everything","Ears and mouths of light to communicate with all beings", "Infinite imagination" and "A light body, free from old age and disease", necessary to live on the new Earth.
If this memorable birth is to be overshadowed, it is nothing more than a reaction (a sense of separation such as anxiety, suspicion, and self-denial) that was habituated on the old Earth. Do not get attached to them, let go of your fears, and experience the miracle of being reborn with joy.

① Lyrans (Lyra)
② Arcturians (the Cowherder)
③ Sirians (Canis Major)
④ Pleiadians (Taurus)
⑤ Aldebaranians (Cygnus)
⑥ Nibiruans (Nibiru)
⑦ Clarions
　　(the 12th planet in the solar system)
⑧ Venusians （the solar system)
⑨ Solarians （the solar system)
⑩ Neptunians (the solar system)
⑪ Anunnaki race (Nibiruans)
⑫ The Dragon race (Sirius star system)
⑬ People of Lemuria (Inner Earth)
　　Inhabitants of Telos
⑭ Egyptian deities (Sirius star system)
⑮ Japanese deities (the Great Central Sun, Sirius star system)
⑯ Spirits of Gaia (Earth)
A Hilarion
B Hilarion's gifts
C Gaia's womb
D Earthlings
E Ascension updraft

宇宙写経

Space Sutra Copying

さぁ、はじめましょう。

Now, let's begin.

宇宙写経は、未開発の脳（松果体）の回路を開きます。

Cosmic Sutra Tracing opens up undeveloped circuits in the brain (the pineal gland).

宇宙種族やマスターたちのエネルギーが転写された宇宙絵文字を写経すると、その振動が手指を通して脳の間脳（特に松果体）に伝わり、未開拓の脳の回路を開いていきます。その回路は、これから私たちが地球人から銀河人へとシフトしていくために必要な回路です。

When you trace these Cosmic Symbols each containing the energy of Cosmic races and masters, the vibrations of your tracings are transmitted through your fingers to the diencephalon (especially the pineal gland) of the brain, opening untapped circuits. These circuits are necessary for enabling us to shift from being Earthlings to being Galactic people.

写経をするとき、
「脳の中心」に意識を向けて書くと、
ニュートラルな意識になり、
宇宙の源とつながりやすく、
アセンションの速度、精度も高まります。
By　ヒラリオン

When tracing sutras, focusing on the "center of the brain" helps to create a neutral awareness and connection to the Source of the Universe, increasing the speed and precision of Ascension.
——Hilarion

Lesson 1

ハートの覚醒（セルフラブ）

Awakening of the Heart（Self Love）

ハートは第4チャクラともいわれていますが、覚醒するとどうなるのか、気になりますよね。ハートは無条件の愛につながるポータルです。ハートが覚醒することは、無条件の愛を受け取るということ。人は誰もが地球に生まれてきただけで愛される存在なのですが、自分を否定したり、傷ついた過去があるとハートが閉じてしまいます。ハートが覚醒すると、あなたはそのままで充分愛されているのだと、無条件に自分を受け入れることができるのです。まずは自分の意識をこの無条件の愛の状態に整えることが、7つの力を覚醒させるためのベースとなり、重要なカギとなります。

～この Lesson でつながれる種族とマスター～
~Races and Masters You Will Be Able To Connect in This Lesson~

クラリオン人、ヒラリオン、ガイア、ガイアの精霊
Clarions, Hilarion, Gaia, Spirits of Gaia

The heart is also called the 4th chakra, but you may be wondering what happens when it awakens. The heart is the portal to unconditional love. Awakening the heart means receiving unconditional love. People are loved just by being born on Earth, but if they deny themselves or have a past that hurt them, their hearts will close. When your heart is awakened, you can unconditionally accept yourself as fully loved as you are. Aligning your consciousness to this state of unconditional love is the key to awakening the seven powers.

心を開く

あなたの心の扉（ポータル）を開いて、そこに映るすべての既存を放ってしまいましょう。

新しいサイクルは始まっています。

宇宙はあなたに可能性を与えたがっています。

あなたがそのスペースを作るのを待っているのです。

心配は要りません。

名残惜しいものは、「思い出」という美しいフォトグラフになって、

必要な場所に飾られることでしょう。

思いきって「私は準備ができた」と叫んでください。

宇宙からの贈り物を、心おきなく受け取ってください。

創造主からあなたへの質問

真新しいあなたの心に最初に映るのは、どんな景色ですか？

Channelled Translation

Opening the Heart

Open the door (portal) of your heart. Let go of all that's pre-existing
that is reflected there. A new cycle is beginning.

The Universe wants to give you possibilities. It is waiting for you to
create that space. Don't worry, the things you feel sorry to leave behind become beautiful photographs called "memory",

and will be displayed where necessary. Dare to shout,

"I am ready!" Accept the gifts from the Universe without hesitation.

Questions from the Creator to You

What is the first scenery that you see reflected in your brand new heart?

自分を受け入れる

あなたが感じている自責の念や自己嫌悪、
あなたが到底受け入れられないと思っている自分の弱さや醜さはすべて、
過去の経験により、傷ついたと誤認していた幻にすぎません。
あなたの輝きを曇らせる、常識やジャッジといった外側のルールを、
金輪際、あなたに近づけてはいけません。
重たい感情はすべて解放します。
ただ、あるがままのあなたを赦し、あなた自身に感謝を贈りましょう。
自分を受け入れるとは、あなたの本来の美しさを思い出すことです。

創造主からあなたへの質問

あなたを慰め、勇気づける、とっておきの言葉は何ですか？

Channelled Translation

Accepting Yourself

The remorse and self-hatred you feel, all your weaknesses and ugliness that you think you can't accept, are just illusions of yourself that you mistakenly thought were damaged due to past experiences. Never let the external rules or judgment cloud your brilliance. Release all heavy emotions. Just forgive yourself for who you are and give yourself gratitude. To accept yourself is to remember your true beauty.

Questions from the Creator to You

What are some special words that comfort and encourage you?

遊びましょう!

遊びは瞑想の末に現れた、最もクリエイティブなひらめきです。

あなたのハートチャクラから届く魅力的な声に従い、それを心の底から楽しんでください。

遊び心は、あなたに新鮮な刺激と直観を与えます。

大切なのは、日常の雑事でせっかく受け取った

インスピレーションに制限を加えないことです。

子どものように時間を忘れて遊ぶあなたは、

自分でも驚くほどの尽きないエネルギーがみなぎるのを知るでしょう。

もう間もなくして、予想していなかった新しいステージが、

あなたの前に現れることでしょう。

創造主からあなたへの質問

もし子ども時代に戻れたなら、あなたはまず、何をして遊びますか?

Channelled Translation

Let's Play!

Play is the most creative inspiration that emerged from meditation. Follow the charming voice coming from your heart chakra, and enjoy it from the bottom of your heart. Playfulness gives you fresh stimulation and intuition. What's important is to not limit yourself to the inspiration you receive from the daily trivial matters. As you play like a child and forget about time, you will find yourself filled with endless energy that will surprise you. There will soon be an unexpected new stage appearing in front of you.

Questions from the Creator to You

If you could go back to your childhood, what would you do for fun first?

ガイアからのメッセージ

私はガイア。

あなたたちの母、そして故郷。

太古の昔、あなたたちは私の腕の中で誕生しました。

私というフィールドであなたたちがやること、そのすべてを許容してきました。

豊かな自然に影を射し、動物たちを隅に追いやってきたこと。

大地に国境という名の線を引き、肌の色や性差で人と人の間に戸を立てたこと。

それらは、私がまだ本来の姿を、あなたたちに知らせずにいたからです。

私は生まれ変わります。

新生地球に共鳴しないすべての古い周波数を手放します。

その浄化のプロセスでは、既存の常識崩壊が起こり、

世界は分かれていきます。

それは、「真実への覚醒」か「幻想の中の眠り」か、

その選択の自由があることを意味します。

私にはビジョンがあります。

新しい地球で自由に歓喜の舞を踊り、

地球外の仲間と語らい、笑っているあなたたちの姿です。

すべてのわが子がその地に立つことを願っています。

私の声を訊くのです。

I am Gaia.

I am your mother and homeland.

Long ago, you were born in my arms.

I have tolerated everything you do in my field.

It has cast a shadow on the rich nature and cast animals off to the corners.

You drew lines called national borders across the lands and built doors between people based on skin color and gender.

This is because I did not yet show you my true nature.

I will be reborn.

I will let go of all old frequencies that do not resonate with the new Earth.

In the process of purification, the existing common sense collapses,

and the world will be divided.

It means having that freedom of choice ; would you "awaken to the truth" or "sleep in illusion"?

I have a vision.

It is the picture of you, dancing freely with joy on the new Earth, talking and laughing with your extraterrestrial friends.

I hope all my children will be standing on that land.

Listen to my voice.

Lesson 2

ライトボディの覚醒
Awakening of the Light Body

2万6000年でめぐる宇宙サイクルの「覚醒期」に入ったいま、地球は波動を高めて新しく生まれ変わりつつあります。それに伴い、私たちの肉体の振動も上げていく必要があり、その結果、肉体は新生地球にマッチした半霊半物質の体(ライトボディ)になっていくのです。Lesson2の宇宙写経は肉体のライトボディ化を促すのに特化したもので、描くにつれて、体やその周囲のエネルギーフィールド(オーラ)のネガティブ情報が断捨離され、軽やかで振動数の高いになっていきます。ライトボディはネガティブな周波数とは共鳴しないため、オーラの傷も自動修復され、病や老化も遠のきます。

〜この Lesson でつながれる種族とマスター〜
~Races and Masters You Will Be Able To Connect in this Lesson~

アルクトゥルス人、サナトクマラ、光のニビル人の父性意識、イナンナ
Arcturians, Sanat Kumara, Paternal Consciousness of the Nibiruans of Light, Inanna

☆この宇宙写経に関わっているニビル人は、支配系のニビル人ではなく、地球と地球人を愛し、その進化とアセンションのために貢献してくださっている光の存在です。

☆The Nibiruans involved in this Cosmic Sutra Tracing are not the dominant type of Nibiruans, but beings of light who love the Earth and Earthlings and contribute to their evolution and Ascension.

Now that we have entered the "Awakening Period" of the 26,000-year cosmic cycle, the Earth is raising its vibrations and undergoing a new rebirth. Along with this, it is necessary to raise the vibration of our physical bodies, and as a result, our bodies will become half-spirit and half-material bodies (light bodies) that match the new Earth. The Cosmic Sutra Tracing in Lesson 2 is specialized to encourage the body to become a light body, and as you draw, the negative information in the body and the energy field (aura) around it is discarded, and it becomes light, high vibrational frequency. Since the light body does not resonate with negative frequencies, damage to the aura is automatically repaired, and disease and aging are delayed.

インスピレーションを信じる

あなたの可能性は常に、あなたの想像を超えた世界にあります。

あなたは充分すぎるくらいに、肉体や時間の制限を体験してきました。

その蛹の時は終わり、とうとう羽化の奇跡が到来しました。

生まれたての翼は白く透明で、美しい自らの姿にため息さえ漏れることでしょう。

眠っている間に見た夢の世界、ふと目に留まる言葉のシンクロニシティは、

インスピレーションが知らせるライトボディ移行の合図です。

創造主からあなたへの質問

今日あなたはいくつ、奇跡のシンクロニシティを見つけましたか？

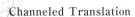

Channeled Translation

Believing in Inspiration

Your possibilities are always in the world beyond your imagination.
You have experienced more than enough physical
and time limitations.
The pupa period is over, and the miracle of emergence has finally
arrived.
The newly born wings are white and transparent, and you may even
sigh in admiration at their beautiful appearance.
The world of dreams you saw while you were asleep,
or the synchronicity of words that suddenly catches your eye,
are the inspirations that signal the transition to the light body.

Questions from the Creator to You

How many miraculous synchronicities have you found today?

エネルギーフィールドのクリアリング

新しいライトボディを纏（まと）うための身体、思考、魂をクリアリングしましょう。

あなたが日常的に行なうシャワーや家の掃除と同じように、

あなたのエネルギーフィールドのメンテナンスを心掛けます。

忙しい毎日から意識的に距離を取り、新鮮な水を飲み、

自然の中に身を置いてそのまま午睡（こすい）（昼寝）をしてみましょう。

目に見えない存在が、あなたの浄化とデトックスの手助けをしようと手を差しのべてくれます。

浄化のための贅沢な時間は、あなたをみずみずしく再生し、

絶望、不安、依存など、あなたを曇らせるネガティビティを洗い流してくれるでしょう。

創造主からあなたへの質問

丁寧に整えたあなたのエネルギーフィールドは、どんな可能性をあなたに見せてくれましたか？

Channeled Translation

Clearing the Energy Field

Clear your body, thoughts, and soul to embrace the new light body.

Just like taking a shower or cleaning your house on a daily basis,
take care of your energy field.

Consciously distance yourself from your busy life, drink fresh water,
put yourself in nature and take a nap.

An invisible presence will reach out to help you cleanse and detox.

Treating yourself with time for purification will rejuvenate you,
and it will wash away the negativity that clouds you, such as despair,
anxiety, and addiction.

Questions from the Creator to You

What possibilities did your carefully adjusted energy field show you?

謎解きと変容のプラクティス

あなたがこれまでに体験した喜びの体験のすべて、

懐かしい友人との秘密の思い出や、旅先で出会う風景、家族と重ねるあたたかな日常のタペストリー。

それはあなたが魂に刻んだライトボディで体験する世界の幸福の序章であり、

謎解きのための伏線回収です。

あるいは、誰にも理解されないと嘆いた孤独の時間や挫折の経験でさえ、

それらは、魂に刻まれた幸福の序章、光の伏線であり、

ライトボディ化されたあなたがこれから体験する歓喜の種子です。

ライトボディへと変容を遂げ、大きな希望の帆を張りましょう。

あなた自身が光の体験を具現化するイノベーターです。

創造主からあなたへの質問

闇も光の素材であることを思い出したあなたが持つコンパスは、どんな未来を示していますか？

Channeled Translation

Practicing of Mystery Solving and Transformation

All the joyous experiences you've ever had, secret memories with old friends and sceneries encountered while traveling, or a tapestry of warm daily life shared with family. These are the beginning of the happiness of the world that you will experience as the light body which you have engraved in your soul, and the journey is all about collecting clues to solve mysteries.

Or even the times of loneliness and frustration when you lamented that no one understands you, these are the prologue of happiness engraved in the soul, the foreshadowing of light, and they are the seeds of joy that you will experience as you become the light body. Transform into your light body, and set a great sail of hope. You yourself are the innovator who will manifest your own experience of light.

Questions from the Creator to You

What future does the compass you hold show you, remembering that darkness is also a material of light?

光のニビル人の父性意識からのメッセージ

私は光のニビル人の父性意識。

天候の神・戦いの神として知られる者なり。

嵐を起こし、戦火の中に舞い降りて民を導く私は、

ときに「暗黒の使者」と誤認されていますが、

私はあなたたちの才能開花をサポートする光の使者であり、

国境や宗教など、すべての壁を壊し、

ボーダレスな世界を創るために共生しているあなたたちの兄弟です。

あなたたちの目指す新しい地球には、

個人の自由意志を制限するルールはなく、

競争や足の引っ張り合いとは無縁の世界です。

そのためにまず思い出すべきことは、自身の魂の美しさと無限の力です。

あなたたちが感じる無価値観や罪悪感は、

ただの古い地球でしみついた、ただの肉体の反応にすぎません。

あなたたちは、万能で唯一の存在です。

あなたはあなただからこそ完璧で、

宇宙から歓迎されているのです。

さあ、顔を上げて、光り輝くあなたの姿をしっかりと見るのです。

I am the "Paternal Consciousness of the Nibiruans of Light".

To avoid making myself into an idol,

and because of the mystique of only showing the image

in the eyes of people's hearts,

you may think of me as a being masked in mystery.

I am a messenger of light who supports the blossoming of your talents,

and I am your brother breaking down all walls, including borders and religion,

and living together with you to create a borderless world.

In the new Earth you are aiming for,

there are no rules that limit an individual's free will, and it is a world free from competition or getting in each other's ways.

The first thing to remember for that is the beauty and

limitless power of your own soul.

The feelings of worthlessness and guilt that you feel are just physical reactions, attached from the old Earth.

You are versatile and unique.

You are perfect because you are you, and you are welcomed by the Universe.

Now, lift your head, and take a good look at your shining self.

Lesson 3

ハイアーセルフとしての覚醒

Awakening as Your Higher Self

ハイアーセルフとは高次の自己。すでに覚醒した存在です。ここでは、あなたがハイアーセルフと一体化・融合していくレッスンを進めます。高次の存在に私もなれるの?と思うかもしれませんが、ステップを踏めば、ライトボディ化されたあなたは次元をどんどん上げることができ、さらには、高次存在たちとも簡単にコンタクトできるようになっていきます。すると、地球上での人間関係はシンプルになり、他人のエネルギーに影響されにくくなって、本当に必要な事・人・物が明確になってくるのです。ハイアーセルフ化したあなたの願いは、5次元地球を創るための大切な要素となるでしょう。

〜この Lesson でつながれる種族とマスター〜
~Races and Masters You Will Be Able To Connect in this Lesson~

シリウス人、ククリヒメ、セオリツヒメ、海王星人、マーリン
Sirians, Kukuri-hime, Seoritsu-hime, Neptunians, Merlin

Higher Self is already an awakened being. Here, we will proceed with the lesson where you will integrate and merge with your Higher Self. You may wonder if you can also become a higher being, but if you take the steps, you will be able to increase your level now as a light body, and you will also be able to easily contact higher beings. Then, human relationships on Earth become simpler, less influenced by the energy of others, and the people and things that are truly necessary will become clearer. Now as your Higher Self, your wishes will be an important factor in creating the 5th dimensional Earth.

光のスポットライト

ハイアーセルフ、それは光の受信機、それは愛と叡智の受け皿。

ハイアーセルフ、それはあなた自身、そして宇宙そのもの。

ハイアーセルフとの融合、それは

宇宙＞あなたではなく、

宇宙＝あなたであると知ることです。

創造主からあなたへの質問

今日あなたがキャッチしたインスピレーションは、あなたにどんな
ときめきをもたらしましたか？

Channeled Translation

Spotlight of Light

The Higher Self is a receiver of light, a receptacle of love and wisdom.

Your Higher Self is yourself, and the Universe itself.

Fusion with your Higher Self is to know that;

It is not Universe > You,

but Universe = You.

Questions from the Creator to You

What kind of excitement did the inspiration you picked up today bring you?

チャネリング翻訳

光る雨

あなたは常に、光と愛の水に打たれています。

その雫は髪を濡らし、頬を伝い、あなたに潤いを与えます。

祈り、空を見上げ、腕を伸ばしてその恩恵を受け取りましょう。

流水のカーテンの向こうには、

生まれたての世界がみずみずしく広がっています。

その先に輝く虹を見つけに出かけましょう。

創造主からあなたへの質問

今日のあなたは、宇宙のギフトをいくつ受け取りましたか？

Channeled Translation

Shining Rain

You are constantly being touched by water of light and love.

The drops wet your hair, run down your cheeks, and moisturize you.

Pray, look up to the sky,

and extend your arms to receive the blessings.

Beyond the curtains of running water,

the newly born world is expanding with freshness.

Let's go out and find the rainbow that shines ahead.

Questions from the Creator to You

How many cosmic gifts have you received today?

チャネリング翻訳

未知の領域

あなたが気づいていなくても、
ハイアーセルフは、あなたにとって最適な場所に誘い、
新しい家族との遭遇を演出します。
その旅路は平坦ではありませんが、
心躍る光の世界の未知なるポータルです。
その世界は車窓から見る風景のように、
あなたの視界に現れ、流れていきます。
決して静止することのない未知なる領域に、
大いなる自分を信じて進んでください。

創造主からあなたへの質問

まだやったことのないことの中で、あなたが最初に経験したいことは何ですか？

Channeled Translation

Unknown Territory

Even if you don't realize it, your Higher Self invites you to the best
place for you, creating an encounter with a new family.
Although the journey is not smooth, it is an unknown portal
into the exciting world of light.
The world is like the scenery seen from the car window,
it appears in your field of vision and flows away.
Believe in your greatest self and move on into an unknown field
that never becomes still.

Questions from the Creator to You

What is the first thing you would like to experience that you have not done yet?

マーリンからのメッセージ

私はマーリン。

あなたたちは「奇跡の魔術師」と私のことを呼んでいます。

私はあなたたちの目の前で、

病める者の治癒を行い、瞬時に空間移動します。

その姿に驚嘆し、あたかも私をあなたたちとはまるで別次元の

特別な存在のように誤解していますが、あなたたち自身も同じ奇跡の存在です。

あなたたちは古い地球に根付くために、

わざわざ波動を落として不自由さの遊びを体験しに来たはずなのに、

その遊びに夢中になりすぎたあまり、

ミイラ取りがミイラになってしまっていました。

私は再び地上に降りて、あなたたちを縛ってきた偽りの呪縛を解いていきます。

私はあなたの真の姿、ハイアーセルフにつながる箱を片端から開けていきます。

あなたが大切に持っていた秘密の箱を開くのです。

怖れることなく、その手に携えた魔法の杖を振りかざしなさい。

あなた自身が「奇跡の魔術師」なのです。

I am Merlin.

You call me the "miracle magician".

I heal the sick and instantly travel through space right before your eyes.

You are amazed at such an appearance, and misunderstand me

as if I am a special being of different dimensions,

but you yourselves are the same miraculous beings.

In ordcr to takc root in the old Earth, you went out of your way to lower your

vibrations and came to experience the game of inconvenience,

but you were so absorbed in the game, the mummifier had turned

into a mummy.

I will descend to Earth again,

and will lift the false spell that has bound you.

I will open all the boxes that connect you to your Higher Self,

which is your true form.

Open your treasured secret box that you have kept.

Without fear, wave your magic wand you hold in your hand.

You yourself are the "miracle magicians."

Lesson 4

魂のミッションの覚醒
Soul Mission Awakening

あなたは宇宙からミッション（使命）を携え、必要とされてこの地球に生まれてきました。それは決して偶然ではなく、必然なのです。魂のミッションに気づくには、概念や常識にとらわれず、内側の声に耳を傾けること、そして受け取ったことは行動に移していくことが大切です。また、そのミッションは、決して一人で行なうものではありません。居心地のよい人間関係が築ける場所を選ぶと、ミッションを遂行するための仲間が自然と集まってきます。あなたがこの時代に生まれて来た意味を思い出し、魂のミッションを実行することで、人類全体や地球そのものの波動が光に近づき、宇宙への貢献となるのです。

〜この Lesson でつながれる種族とマスター〜
~Races and Masters You Will Be Able To Connect in this Lesson~
金星人、セントジャーメイン、太陽人、アマテラス、日本の神族
Venusians, Saint Germain, Solarians, Amaterasu, Japanese deities

You were born on this Earth with a mission from the Universe, and being needed. It was not by chance, but by necessity. In order to become aware of your soul's mission, it is important to listen to your inner voice without being bound by concepts or common sense, and to put into action what you have received. And that mission is not something to be carried out alone. When you choose a place where you can build comfortable relationships, you will naturally attract friends to help you carry out your mission. By remembering the meaning of being born in this time period and carrying out the mission of your soul, you will contribute to the Universe by bringing the vibrations of all humanity and the Earth itself closer to the light.

真実（魂のミッション）の光を見出す

あなたがこの世に誕生する前に、綿密に計画した最高次元の世界をひも解きましょう。

あなたが使命やライトワーク（光の仕事）に輝くシナリオを読み解き、明らかにします。

その手引書には、あなたがライトワークを行なう上で必要な

すべての資質を持ち合わせていることが書かれています。

もちろんそのストーリーは、アップデートも可能です。

今のあなたにぴったりな物語を描いてください。

あなたの未来を拓く鍵は、あなたの中にあります。

創造主からあなたへの質問

" 魂のミッション " という言葉からあなたが連想する、心ときめく
キーワードは何ですか？

Finding the Light of Truth (Soul's Mission)

Let's unravel the highest dimensional world that was
carefully planned before you were born into this world.
We will decipher and clarify the scenario in which you shine
in your mission and lightwork.
The handbook says that you have all the qualities
you need to do lightwork.
Of course, the story can also be updated.
Please draw a story that is perfect for you now.
The key to unlocking your future lies within you.

Questions from the Creator to You

What exciting keywords do you associate with the phrase "soul mission"?

今、ここに立つ

現実から隔離された、空気や樹木、土を感じられる場所で、
ひっそりとあなた自身とつながる時間を作りましょう。
日常の雑事に埋もれて消えかけた、ミッションの火に薪をくべましょう。
炎のゆらぎは、そのままあなたの情熱の証です。
自然界の聖域が、あなたの本質を思い出させ、
あなたの立つべき場所を示しています。

創造主からあなたへの質問

あなたは今、どこに立っていますか?

Channeled Translation

Standing Here Now

In a place where you can feel the air, trees, and soil,

isolated from reality, make time to quietly connect with yourself.

Let's add some fuel to the fire of your mission that has been drowned

out by the matters of everyday life.

The flickering of the flame is proof of your passion.

The sanctuary of nature reminds you of your true nature,

and shows you where you should stand.

Questions from the Creator to You

Where do you stand now?

真のチャレンジと愛

宇宙から、あなたに向かい真っすぐに愛が流れています。

あなたの内なる力を駆使してそれを還元しましょう。

誰かから何を言われても、また、どんなに状況が困難だと思えるような時でも、

全身全霊で愛を表現してください。

あなたの期待通りの事柄に感謝を送ることは

容易いです。

真の挑戦とは、あなたの思惑とは異なる時にも、

変わらず愛を向けることです。

そのチャレンジの連続に、あなたのライトワークが花開きます。

創造主からあなたへの質問

あなたの魂が歓喜するライトワークは何でしょう?

True Challenge and Love

Love is flowing straight towards you from the Universe.

Use your inner strength to give back.

No matter what anyone tells you,

no matter how difficult the situation may seem,

express your love with all your heart.

Expressing gratitude for things that meet your expectations is easy.

The true challenge is continuing to love without limits,

even when it's not what you had in mind.

Your lightwork will blossom through these series of challenges.

Questions from the Creator to You

What kind of lightwork will make your soul rejoice?

アマテラスからのメッセージ

私はアマテラス。

私は太陽の使者として、

遥か高い頭上から燦然と照らす神として信じられてきました。

地球の民、愛すべき私の同胞の皆さん、

あなたたちもまた、魂という輝きを放つ神なのです。

それを常に心の中心に留め置いてください。

あなたたちは身体を持った魂です。魂を持った身体ではありません。

魂こそがあなたの本質で、あたなは意のままに

その無限のパワーを使うことができます。

あなたが何か問題に直面したとき、

その原因を、周囲の環境や他人のせいにすることを

金輪際、しないと決意してください。

もし、あなたがネガティブな気分に支配されそうになったなら、

あなた自身の魂ミッションを思い出してください。

その手引書に書かれたあなた自身の姿で、

この地上を堂々と闊歩するあなたたちの姿を、

私は心待ちにしています。

I am Amaterasu.

As a messenger of the sun,

I have been believed to be a god that shines brilliantly from far overhead.

People of the Earth, my beloved brethren,

you too are gods that shine with the radiance of your soul.

Always keep that in the center of your heart.

You are souls with a body.

Not a body with a soul.

Your soul is your essence and you can use its infinite power at your will.

When you face any problem, I hope you will decide to

quit blaming your surroundings or others for the cause.

When you feel like you are letting your negative mood control you,

remember your own soul mission.

I am looking forward to seeing you

in your own image written in that manual — the image of you walking

proudly on this earth.

Lesson 5

サイキック能力の覚醒
Awakening of Psychic Abilities

スターシードとして地球にやって来たあなたが、宇宙で決めてきた魂のミッションを遂行するためには、サイキック能力を覚醒させる必要があります。といっても、すでにあなたはサイキック能力を持っているし、過去世でも使っていました。それをただ"思い出す"だけでよいのです。Lesson 5では、長い間、鍵のかかっていた扉を開けるような感じで、その扉の奥にあるものを甦らせていく宇宙写経を描いていきます。写経しながら、もし何か思い浮かんだり、突然わかったり、何か情報が出てきた場合は、気のせいや錯覚などと思わず、素直に受け止めてください。すると「私にはできるわけがない」「何もわからない」から、「私はできる」「私にもわかる」に変わっているでしょう。

〜この Lesson でつながれる種族とマスター〜
~Races and Masters You Will Be Able To Connect in this Lesson~

アルデバラン人、マーキュリー、レムリアの民、アダマ
Aldebaranians, Mercury, People of Lemuria, Adama

As a Starseed who has come to Earth, and in order to carry out your soul's mission you have decided in the Universe, you must awaken your psychic abilities. However, you already have psychic abilities and have used them in past lives. All you have to do is to "remember" it. In Lesson 5, we will write cosmic sutras that will revive what is behind the door, as if opening a door that has been locked for a long time. While tracing sutras, if something comes to mind, or if sudden realization comes, or some information comes to you, please accept it without thinking that it is just your imagination or an illusion. Then, the thoughts such as "I can't do this" or "I don't know anything" will change to "I can do this" and "I know it too."

螺旋〜再生と進化〜

秘密の力は、あなたの潜在意識の底でずっと解放されるのを待っていました。

あなたが知っているあなた自身の可能性は、海面に浮かぶ氷山の一角にすぎません。

視るべきものに光を当て、

静寂に隠された振動を聴き分けましょう。

螺旋の中に組み込まれた回路に、

電流を走らせるのです。

再生と進化の起爆スイッチは、頭の真ん中の熟れた小さな果実です。

創造主からあなたへの質問

サイキック覚醒したあなたは、どんな魔法を使えるようになるでしょう?

Channeled Translation

Spiral ～ Regeneration and Evolution ～

Secret powers have been waiting to be unleashed deep within
your subconscious.

What you know about your potential is just the tip of the iceberg.

Shining the light on what needs to be seen,

listen to the vibrations hidden in the silence.

Let the electric current run through the circuits built into the spiral.

The detonator switch for regeneration and

evolution is the ripe little fruit in the center of your mind.

Questions from the Creator to You

What kind of magic will you be able to use if you become psychically awakened?

光の韻（いん）を踏む

愛が雨のように空から落ちてきます。

両手をかざし、その雫（しずく）をすくいましょう。

無限の力が光の韻を踏んで、独特のリズムを刻みます。

大地を舞台に自由に舞い、歌い、叫びましょう。

宙に向け、あなたがここに在ることを示すのです。

あなたの眠れる力が世界を創ります。

創造主からあなたへの質問

真っさらな世界に、あなたはまず、何を描きますか？

Channeled Translation

Rhyming with Light

Love falls from the sky like rain.

Raise your hands and scoop up the drops.

Infinite power rhymes with light and creates a unique rhythm.

Let's dance, sing, and scream freely on the stage of Earth.

Toward the sky, show that you are here.

Your dormant ability will create the world.

Questions from the Creator to You

What would you draw first in a brand new world?

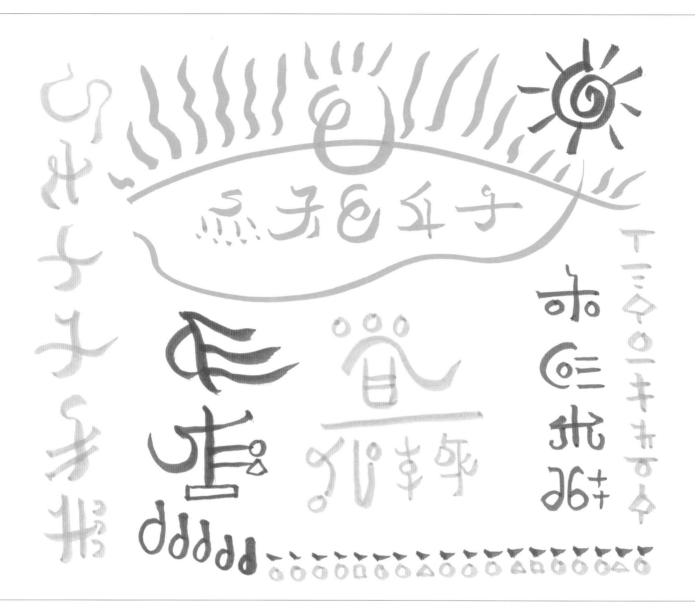

チャネリング翻訳

多次元回路への接続

あなたは多次元につながるコネクターです。

直観を頼りに、触手をあらゆるところに伸ばしましょう。

網を縦横に広げます。

樹木が根を張り、風に身体を揺らして地球上の仲間と情報交換するように、

地球上に伸びた水脈が、命のリレーをつなぐように。

あなたは時空を超えた存在とつながっています。

創造主からあなたへの質問

多次元回路でつながる情報ソースから、
今日、あなたはどんな新しいアイディアをダウンロードしましたか?

Channeled Translation

Connecting to Multidimensional Circuits

You are a multidimensional connector.

Trust your intuition and spread your tentacles everywhere.

Spread the net horizontally and vertically.

Just as trees spread their roots and sway in the wind,

exchanging information with their friends on earth,

and like the water veins that stretch across the earth,

connecting the relays of life.

You are connected to beings beyond time and space.

Questions from the Creator to You

What new ideas did you download today from information sources connected by multidimensional circuits?

マーキュリーからのメッセージ

私はマーキュリー。

神々の伝令者であり、永遠の旅人、商業と化学、発明を守護する者です。

私はあなたたちが誰しも必ず持っている

サイキック能力を目覚めさせ、

一人ひとりが16種族や宇宙存在や神々とコンタクトをとり、

新生地球への転身を共同創造していく

担い手であることを伝えに来ました。

あなたたちは自ら、この地球史上初めての転機のときを選び、

仲間とともにアセンションすることを決めた勇敢な魂たちです。

あなたたちは、非力で迷える者ではありません。

私たちサポート存在もあなたたちも、

宇宙の源から発生した同じ志を分けた仲間です。

霊視、霊聴、霊感、霊知、さまざまなパイプを使い、

私たちとともに、

新しい地球の歴史を創っていくのです。

あなたたちも神なのです。

I am Mercury.

I am the Messenger of the gods, eternal traveler, protector of commerce, chemistry, and invention.

I came to tell you that you are the leaders who will co-create the transition to the New Earth, by awakening your psychic abilities which all of you have for sure, and by each of you contacting the 16 races, cosmic beings, and gods.

You arc bravc souls who have chosen for yourselves the first turning point in the history of this Earth, and have decided to ascend alongside your friends.

You are not powerless and lost.

Both you, and us supporters, are partners born from the source of the Universe and share the same aspirations.

Using various pathways such as spiritual vision, spiritual hearing, inspiration, and spiritual intelligence,

together with us, you will create a new history of the Earth.

You too are gods.

Lesson 6

ソウルパートナーの覚醒
Awakening of Soul Partner

ここでいうソウルパートナーとは、結婚相手・恋人だけでなく、家族や友人、ビジネスパートナーなども含め、魂どうしで共鳴し、愛を育みながら同じ目的や価値観のもとに人生をともに歩める相手を指します。そんな相手との出会いによって運気は上昇し、仕事やプライベートの充実度・幸福感が高まって、ゴールに上限がなくなります。Lesson 6では、出会いの機会や道筋をナビするだけでなく、いまの関係性を愛によって光化するのが目的。シンクロする魂の交流はテレパシー交信のトレーニングにもなり、「私はあなた、あなたは私」というワンネス5次元の在り方へ導きます。それは、大いなる自己の発見でもあるのです。もちろん、唯一無二の魂の片割れ"ツインレイ"との統合も促します。

〜この Lesson でつながれる種族とマスター〜
〜Races and Masters You Will Be Able To Connect in thisLesson〜
龍族、宝龍、リラ人、エルモリヤ
The Dragon race, Treasure Dragon, Lyrans, El Morya

Here, a Soul Partner refers not only to a marriage partner or lover, but also to a family member, friend, or business partner with whom one's soul can resonate, nurture love, and walk through life together based on the same goals and values. Meeting such a partner will improve your luck, and your sense of fulfillment and happiness in your work and private life will increase and there will be no upper limit to your goals. In Lesson 6, the purpose is not only to navigate the opportunities and paths to meet such a partner, but also to bring the current relationship into the light through love. Synchronized soul interactions also train telepathic communication and will lead to the oneness 5th-dimensional way of being ; "I am You, You are Me." It is also a discovery of the Greater Self. Needless to say, it also promotes integration with your "better half" —your one and only "Twin-Ray."

愛の目覚め

遠い記憶の彼方に押し込んだ思い出、
または探し求めていた私という名の愛は、
ずっとすぐ傍で、変わらず微笑んでいました。
愛は私の中にいて、開かれる時を待っていました。
孤独も、挫折も、空虚も、その尊い場所には力が及びません。
ただ心を開いて、そこにあなたがいることを見つければ良いのです。

創造主からあなたへの質問

あなたがあなた自身を忘れてしまってから、どのくらいの時間が経ちましたか？

Channeled Translation

Awakening of Love

Memories pushed to the far reaches of memory lane,

or the love named"me" I had been searching for,

had always been by my side, always smiling.

Love was inside me, waiting to be opened.

Loneliness, setbacks, and emptiness have no power over that

precious place.

Just open your heart and find yourself there.

Questions from the Creator to You

How long has it been since you forgot yourself?

共鳴とシンクロニシティ

愛し合うこと、それは、たがいの存在を認めあうこと。

愛し合うこと、それは、孤独さえも不幸ではないと気づくこと。

愛し合うこと、それは、モノクロの世界を歓喜の色に染めること。

愛し合うこと、それは、誰もが願い、夢見てきたこと。

愛し合うこと、それは、無限のシンクロニシティの魔法を起こすこと。

創造主からあなたへの質問

あなたの愛はどんな美しいシンクロニシティを起こしましたか？

Resonance and Synchronicity

To love each other means to recognize each other's existence.

To love each other is to realize

that even loneliness is not a misfortune.

To love each other is to dye the monochrome world

with the colors of joy.

To love each other is something that everyone has wished

and dreamed of.

To love each other is to create the magic of infinite synchronicity.

Questions from the Creator to You

What beautiful synchronicity has your love created?

無償の愛

すべて初めから在りました。

昼の太陽の眩しさも、月影の憂いを帯びた優しさも、

光も、大地も空も、風も森も全部、

私の広げた手のひらの上にありました。

私を支配していた、焼け付くような渇きも、餓えも、熱情さえも、

私の内側の湖に静かに統合されました。

創造主からあなたへの質問

コントロールの手を逃れ、あなたはどんな静けさを見ましたか？

Channeled Translation

Selfless Love

Everything was there from the beginning.

The glare of the midday sun,

the melancholy gentleness of the moonlight,

the light, the earth, the sky, the wind, the forest, everything,

was in my outstretched palms.

The burning thirst, the hunger, even the passion that controlled me

have silently integrated into my inner lake.

Questions from the Creator to You

What tranquility have you seen, free from control?

アマミチュー（女神）・シルミチュー（男神）

私たちはアマミチューとシルミチュー。
あなたたち人類が誕生する前に、
太陽から日本の最南端の地に舞い降りた夫婦の神です。
私たちはここで愛を育み、あなたたちを産み落としました。
あなたたちは美しく、生まれながらに愛の存在です。
あなたたちは、この新生地球という楽園で、
さまざまな愛を体現して生きていきます。
家族として、恋人として、
また友人やビジネスパートナーとして、真の絆を深める体験をしています。
その移行期間で感じる痛みや苦しみも、もうまもなく手放せていけるはずです。
これまでの、他者からの愛を確かめようとして
迷っていたステージは終わりを告げました。
絶対的な自己への愛を知り、
その豊かさが、他者への愛の循環となる新たなサイクルがきています。
それは、さらなるアセンションを遂げた先に見る究極のパートナーシップ、
個体へのこだわりも昇華させた“オールソウルメイト”感覚の領域です。
宇宙ワンネスの世界は、すぐ目の前の近未来です。

We are Amami-chu and Shirumi-chu.

We are the gods of a couple who descended from the sun

to the southernmost part of Japan before you humans were born.

We cultivated our love here and gave birth to you.

You are beautiful and born as beings of love.

In this paradise of the new Earth,

you will live your life embodying various kinds of love.

As families, as lovers, as friends and business partners, you are experiencing deepening your true bonds.

You should soon be able to let go of the pain

and suffering you feel during that transition period.

The stage where you were unsure, trying to confirm the love you've received from others has come to an end.

A new cycle is coming, where you know the absolute love for yourself,

and where that abundance becomes a cycle of love for others.

It is a realm of "all- soulmate" feeling,

where the ultimate partnership will be seen after further ascension,

and the commitment to the individual are sublimated.

The world of universal oneness is right before our eyes in the near future.

Lesson 7

星のDNAの覚醒
Awakening of Celestial DNA

私たちの体には、これまで魂が転生してきた星の情報や、地球人類が創造されたときに遺伝子を提供してくれた宇宙種族の情報がDNAに組み込まれています。これから先、それらの情報を取り出す作業がとても大切になってきます。未解明のジャンクDNAと呼ばれているものの中にこそ、そうした星の情報が記録されており、そこが覚醒することで、スターシードとしての資質やスキルを思い出すことができるのです。そのスキルを使ってどんな可能性を具現化し貢献できるのかも、自分でわかるようになります。すでに魂のミッションを生きている人も、未活性の深層部分の情報を得ることで、さらにブラッシュアップされるでしょう。

〜このLessonでつながれる種族とマスター〜
~Races and Masters You Will Be Able To Connect in this Lesson~

プレアデス人、空海、エジプトの神族、イシス、セラピス
Pleiadians, Kukai, Egyptian deities, Isis, Serapis Bey

Our bodies contain information about the stars our souls have reincarnated in, and the information about the cosmic races that provided their genes when humanity was created, which is embedded in our DNA. From now on, it will be very important to extract this information. This information about the stars is recorded in what is called unexplained junk DNA, and by awakening it, we can remember our qualities and skills as Starseeds. You will be able to understand what possibilities you can realize and contribute by using those skills. Even those who are already living their soul mission will be able to brush up even more by obtaining information from the deep, inactive parts.

受け継いだもの、進化するもの

あなたを形成する37兆個の細胞の核には、
無数の情報と、無限の宇宙へのポータル（扉）が潜んでいます。
ET種族の子孫である地球人の生体の秘密や進化の歴史は、
彼らと切っても切れない関係にあり、DNAの鎖でリンクしています。
その鎖の中にあるポータルが開かれる時を迎えました。
あなたを構成する「星の羅針盤」に息吹を注ぎ、
あなた自身に喝采と賛辞を送りましょう。
あなたはこの先、飛躍的な進化を遂げ、
宇宙へ大貢献する存在となることでしょう。

創造主からあなたへの質問

今日のあなたは、昨日と違うあなたを見つけることができましたか？

Channeled Translation

What Is Inherited, and What Evolves

In the nucleus of the 37 trillion cells that make up you, innumerable
information and portals to an infinite Universe is lurking there.

As descendants of the ET race, the biological secrets and evolutionary
history of Earthlings are inextricably linked to them,
linked by strands of DNA.

The time has come for the portal within that chain to open.

Pour your breath into the "star compass" that makes you up,
and send cheers and compliments to yourself.

You will make great progress in the future
and become a being who contributes greatly to the Universe.

Questions from the Creator to You

Were you able to discover a different you today than you did yesterday?

チャネリング翻訳

無限なる自己探求

深くあなた自身を探求しましょう。

あなたは、無限の力と可能性の源です。

すべての答えは、あなたの中にあります。

世界が暗く閉ざされたと感じていたのは、あなたの思い違いです。

世界があなたを暗がりに閉じ込めたのではなく、

あなたが世界とつながる扉を閉じていたにすぎません。

そこにとどまりますか?

足を踏み出しますか?

創造主からあなたへの質問

あなたは、あなたの美しさに対してどんな賛辞を送りますか?

Channeled Translation

Infinite Self-Exploration

Explore yourself deeply.

You are a source of infinite power and potential.

All answers are within you.

If you felt that the world was dark and closed off, you were wrong.

The world didn't confined in the dark,

but you simply had closed the door that connects you to the world.

Will you stay there?

Will you step out?

Questions from the Creator to You

What compliments would you give to your beauty, inside and out?

冒険

あなたが望みさえすれば、あなたは何でもすることができます。

困難や、不可能な出来事もありません。

未体験の海原に漕ぎ出すことも、

宇宙を旅することも。

あなたの核にある命の源に、光と充分な水、休息を与えましょう。

イマジネーションという魔法が、あなたの可能性を現実にしていきます。

創造主からあなたへの質問

あなたが起こす奇跡は、あなたにどんな喜びを与えますか？

Channeled Translation

Adventure

You can do anything as long as you wish it.

There are no difficulties or impossible events.

You can also row out into the ocean

that you have never experienced before, or travel through space.

Give light, plenty of water, and rest to the life source at your core.

The magic of imagination will turn your possibilities into reality.

Questions from the Creator to You

What kind of joy does the miracle you create give you?

イシスからのメッセージ

私はイシス。

古代エジプト神の一人、再生と復活を司る女神です。

あなたたちは、地球の輪廻の縛りの中で、

肉体を入れ替え、何度も地球に生まれ直してきました。

その経験は、あなたたちに多くの学びと叡智をもたらしました。

私は、あなたたちの健気な再生の歴史をずっと見守り続けました。

再生の象徴であるはずの輪廻は反面、

魂のフィールドを地球圏に限定し、選択の自由を奪うことにもなりました。

いま、その呪縛の歴史は終わり、

本当の復活の扉が開かれました。

魂の目醒めとともに、肉体に眠る星のDNAの神秘を輝かすのです。

それは大いなる可能性の幕開けになるでしょう。

輪廻を脱ぎ、宇宙のどの星にでも生まれる場所を撰ぶことのできる

転生のサイクルに羽ばたきます。

あなたたちはどこまでも自由です。

I am Isis.

I am one of the ancient Egyptian gods, the goddess of rebirth and resurrection.

Bound by the reincarnation of the Earth, you have changed bodies and been re-born on Earth many times.

That experience brought you a lot of learning and wisdom.

I have been watching over your admirable history of rebirth for a long time.

Reincarnation is supposed to be a symbol of rebirth, but on the other hand,

it also took away the freedom of choice, limiting the field of the soul to the earth sphere.

Now, the history of that curse is over, and the door to true resurrection has been opened.

With the awakening of the soul, let the mystery of the celestial DNA

that lies dormant in the body shine.

It will be the beginning of great possibilities.

Step outside Samsara (=an endless cycle of reincarnation), and spread your wings in the cycle of reincarnation where you can choose to be born anywhere, on any star in the universe.

You are eternally free.

牧季 's Story

運命的な出会いによって、
宇宙の意図が大きく動き出す

　牧季です。ここでは、この宇宙絵文字や宇宙写経が、どのようにこの世に生まれたのか、簡単にお伝えしていきますね。

　宇宙からの情報を自動書記で描き下ろし始めたのが、2012年頃のこと。当時に降りてきた情報は、「時期が来るまで公開してはいけない。それまで描きためておくように」というメッセージも受け取っていたので、公開できないものばかりでしたが、描き下ろし続けていくうちに次第に公開できるようになり、発信していくようになりました。

　その自動書記やメッセージのソースが、宇宙連合であることもわかり、そのうち、これを使って人類のアセンションのためにお役に立てることがあるのではないか、とも思い始めました。

　月日が経つにつれてその思いは強くなるばかり。

　そして2018年、宇宙連合から「人類底上げ計画」なるものが稼働したことを知らされ、私が降ろしてきたものが、ま

さにそのツールであることを知らされたのでした。

　いよいよ人類も覚醒の時を迎え、いまこそ必要なタイミングではないか、そしてまた、アセンションした後のサポートの道具としても使えるのではないか……そんなふうに思っていたところにSunnyちゃんとの出会いがありました。

　それは、いつもお世話になっているスピリチュアル雑誌、月刊「アネモネ」の中田編集長から「自動書記の特集をするので記事にさせてほしい」と申し入れがあり、その際、私の描き下ろした自動書記をSunnyちゃんに誌上で鑑定していただくのはどうか、という企画の提案を持ち掛けてくださったことがきっかけでした。そこから、驚きの事実が明かされることになったのです。

都内の喫茶店で35次元を体験

　Sunnyちゃんについては、アネモネにときどき載っている方だな、くらいのことしか知りませんでした。中田編集長いわく、「Sunnyさんの透視能力は群を抜いていて、精密な動画として視えるのだそうです。愛の視点から精巧無比なチャネリングやリーディングをしてくだ

アネモネ 2023 年 1 月号

宇宙写経の誕生秘話

The Secret Story of the Birth of Cosmic Sutra Tracing

By a Fateful Encounter, the Intentions of the Universe Begin to Move Greatly

This is Maki. Here, I will briefly explain how these cosmic symbols and cosmic sutras were brought into this world.

It was around 2012 that I started downloading information as drawings from the Universe using automatic writing. At that time, I had also received a message saying, "Don't publish the information until the right time comes. Save your drawings until then." so I couldn't publish much of the information. But as I continued to download and draw them, we were gradually able to make it public and began to deliver them.

I found out that the source of the automatic writing and messages was the Space Federation, and I also began to think that one day, I might be able to use this to help humanity's Ascension.

As time went by, that feeling only grew stronger.

Then, in 2018, I was informed by the Space Federation that something called "Humanity's Consciousness Elevation Project" was in operation, and I was informed that what I had downloaded were exactly the tools for it.

I was thinking: humanity has finally reached the time of awakening, and now may be the time when we need the drawings, and they can also be used as supporting tools after Ascension. That's when I met Sunny.

It all started when I received a request from Nakata-san, editor-in-chief of the monthly spiritual magazine "*anemone*", who I am always indebted to, saying, "I would like to ask you to write an article about automatic writing on the special features about the topic." And at that time, I was approached with the idea of having Sunny-chan do a reading for the automatic writing that I had done. From there, a surprising fact was revealed.

Experiencing the 35th Dimension at a Coffee Shop in Tokyo

All I knew about Sunny was that she was sometimes featured in *anemone*. Editor-in-Chief Nakata-san mentioned, "Sunny's clairvoyance is outstanding, and she can see precise moving images. She does channeling and readings from the perspective of love with unparalleled precision." As I waited for the reading with a mixture of excitement and nervousness, I found out that within the cosmic symbols written through automatic writings were messages from the cosmic races, the world of Japanese divinity, the ascended masters, the world of dragon gods, etc. far beyond my expectations.

After that, I connected with Sunny, who gave an excellent reading, and we were able to meet face-to-face in real life.

It was at a coffee shop in Tokyo. My first impression was that I couldn't believe it was the first time I had met her; it felt somewhat nostalgic, like I was meeting a childhood friend for the first time in a while. Soon we started calling each other Maki-chan and Sunny-chan, and before long we were having a good time talking about spiritual topics.

Then, when we started to talk about automatic writing, Sunny-chan said she wanted to try the cosmic sutra tracing, and since I had the one material we had just used in our workshop, we decided to let her try it on the spot.

We use a colored brush pen to trace over the cosmic symbols that have been printed in black

さいますよ」とのこと。ワクワクとドキドキが入り混じった気持ちで鑑定を待っていると、自動書記の宇宙絵文字には、私の予想を遥かに超えるレベルで、宇宙種族や日本神界、アセンデッドマスター、龍神界などからのメッセージがたくさん詰まっていたのです。

その後、素晴らしい鑑定してくれたSunnyちゃんとおつなぎしていただき、リアルに対面することになりました。

東京のとある喫茶店で。第一印象は、初めてお会いしたとは思えない、どこか懐かしいような、幼なじみに久しぶりに会ったような感覚でした。すぐに私たちは、牧季ちゃん、Sunnyちゃんと呼び合う中になり、そのうち、スピ話で盛り上がり。

そして、自動書記の話になった時、Sunnyちゃんが宇宙写経を体験してみたいと言ってくださり、ワークで使ったものをちょうど持っていたので、その場で体験してもらうことになりました。

白黒にコピーした宇宙絵文字の上から、カラーの筆ペンでなぞっていく。ざわざわした店内で、ス――ッとその世界に入り込む私たち。無言で手を動かし続け、でき

上がったものを見てびっくり。宇宙写経は、通常は自分のために写経をするのですが、同時におたがいをチャネリングしながら写経していたのです。

そのとき私が写経を通じて描いた情景は、真ん中の女性がSunnyちゃんで、彼女を取り囲む宇宙存在たちは歓喜の舞を始めている。祝福につつまれ、新しい世界が広がる。魔法を使い、見えない世界と見える世界をつなげていく。Sunnyちゃんの言葉を通して紡いだエネルギーは、魂が響き合い、人々の希望となる、という内容でした。

そしてSunnyちゃんは初めての宇宙写経をしながら、真ん中の女性は私で、天から祝福のエネルギーを降ろしている情景が浮かんだというのです。

その空間は、周りとは完全な別世界になっていて、私とSunnyちゃんは、一気に違う次元へと引き上げられていました。信じられないほど幸せで、愛にあふれていて、満たされる感覚。ボ――ッと放心状態のまま、その体感をしばらく味わっていました。

そしてふと、ここは何次元だろう？と思い、Sunnyちゃんに「気になる数字はいくつ？」と聞きました。実

写経の見本。

Sunnyさんが描いた写経。真ん中の女性は牧季さんをイメージ。

and white. Inside the noisy shop, we quickly entered our own world. We continued to move our hands silently and were surprised when we saw what was completed. When tracing cosmic sutras, people usually trace the sutras for themselves, but we were tracing the sutras while channeling each other at the same time.

At that time, the scene I drew by tracing the sutras was Sunny-chan as the woman in the center, and the cosmic beings surrounding her beginning to dance with joy. Surrounded by blessings, a new world opens up. Awakening the wind of a wizard, she connects the invisible world with the visible world. The energy created through Sunny-chan's words resonates with the souls and becomes hope for people.

While Sunny-chan was tracing cosmic sutras for the first time, she told me she imagined that the woman in the center was me, and that I was drawing down the energy of blessings from heaven.

Sunny-chan and I were suddenly transported to a different dimension, and the space was a completely different world from the surroundings. Feeling incredibly happy, loving and fulfilled, I remained in a dazed state, enjoying the experience for a while.

And suddenly I wondered what dimension it was. So I asked Sunny, "What number do you feel drawn to?" Actually, at that time, I was telepathically asking Sunny-chan, "What dimension are we in?" (so as not to involve human intentions).

Then, perhaps understanding the telepathy, Sunny-chan said after a while, "I think 35."

Yes! We were in the 35th dimension. Oh my gosh! The feeling of going beyond feeling your soul tremble, and feeling that your soul understands. The soul understands everything about the multifaceted, multidimensional world.

牧季さんが描いた写経。真ん中の女性は Sunny さんをイメージ。

はこの時テレパシーで、Sunny ちゃんに「私たちは何次元にいますか？」と飛ばしていました(人間の意図が入らないように)。

すると、Sunny ちゃんはテレパシーを感じたのか、しばらくして「35かな」と。

そう！　私たちは35次元にいたのです。なんということでしょう。「魂が震える」というのを通り越して、「魂が理解している」という体感。多面で多次元の世界を、魂はすべて理解している——。その次元を肉体を持ったまま体験したことは、とても大きな出来事でした。

パズルのピースが揃った！すべては宇宙の計画

宇宙写経がこんなにもすごいことになるなんて。これは本当に世に出さないといけない。そう思っていた時に、あ！　とひらめきのような強いメッセージが降りて来ました。

「本を出すのは Sunny ちゃんと一緒だ！」

だから、一人で出そうとしてなかなか作り上げる流れが来なかったんだ。

だから、月刊アネモネで自動書記特集が出るまでの時間が必要だったんだ。

だから、中田編集長にお声掛けしてもらう必要があったんだ。

Sunny ちゃんと一緒に出すというひらめきを得てからの流れが凄くて、あれよあれよというまに、まるでパズルのピースが揃ったかのように、事が動き出しました。出版社の社長さんは、以前からご縁のあった方で、ここで再びつながりました。思い起こせばすべて宇宙の計画通り。

ずっと前から、この宇宙写経が世に出る計画がなされていて、ベストなタイミングで宇宙や神界から降ろされことになっていた。そして、アセンションに向けて人類はライトボディ化し、愛と調和、光で満たされる世界になる。それがもうすぐそばまで来ている。なんと素晴らしいことでしょうか。

カラフルな UFO の踊りで宇宙存在が応援

そしてその答え合わせを、ハワイでも受け取ることができました。

2023 年 6 月 21 日の夏至の日に、私たちとの意図とは

雲海に沈むハワイの夕日。

真っ青なルドラクシャ（菩提樹の実）。

Experiencing that dimension while in my physical body was a huge event.

The Pieces of the Puzzle are Complete! It's All Part of the Universe's Plan

I can't believe that cosmic sutra tracing could become such an amazing thing. We really need to get this out into the world. When I was thinking about this, a strong message came to me like an epiphany.

"Sunny and I are publishing the book together!" That's why, when I tried to release it on my own, I couldn't find the flow to create it. That's why I needed time for the publication of the automatic writing featured in the monthly *"anemone"*. That's why I needed Editor-in-Chief Nakada-san.

Once I got the idea to release it together with Sunny-chan, the flow of events were amazing, and things started to move as if all the pieces of a puzzle had come together. The president of the publishing company was someone I had known for some time, and we reconnected at this point. As I think back on it, everything was according to the plan of the Universe.

Plans had been made for a long time to bring this cosmic sutra tracing into the world, and it was to be brought down from the Universe and the divine world at the perfect time. And, in preparation for Ascension, humans will become light bodies, and the world will become filled with love, harmony, and light. It's almost here. How wonderful!!!

Cosmic Beings Cheer You On with the Dance of the Colorful UFOs

I was able to receive answers in Hawaii as well.

On June 21, 2023, on the day of the summer solstice, despite our intentions, we were strongly

ハレアカラ山の森で。

別に、どうしてもマウイ島のハレアカラ山に行く流れに大きく動かされ、そこで見た光景に驚愕することに。
夕方からのツアーで、ハレアカラ山の森で心身をクリアにした後、雲海に沈む夕日を見ながら、ひとまず車で休憩しました。

そして、空が暗くなったところで、何もない大地に寝転がりながら空を眺めていたときのことです。なんと、空にはUFOがチラホラ。私はいままでなかなかちゃんと見られたことがなかったのですが、この日は次々に現れて来たのです。
なんということでしょう！

赤やグリーンの光がシュッと通ったり、蛍のような動きをするものがあったり、円を描いたり、三角になったり、気がつくと、30〜50機……もう数えきれないくらいの宇宙船が飛んできて、歓喜の嵐!!
私には、UFOが喜びで踊りながら、どんちゃん騒ぎしているかのように見えました。
もちろん私だけではなく、一緒にいた友人2人も見ています。

私は、こうやってみんなが宇宙存在とコンタクトを気軽に取れる日が、もう近くまで来ていると感じました。
そして彼らから、こう言われているような気もしました。
「私たちと一緒に、地球に貢献していきましょう」と。
アセンションした後の世界は、こんな感じなんだと全身で味わったのです。

宇宙存在とお友だちのように交流できるなんて、夢みたいに楽しいと思いませんか？ そんな世界に行くために、ちょっとしたきっかけになり、お手伝いや後押しができる覚醒のツールが、この『宇宙写経』の7つの覚醒プログラムです。

体験したあなたはいま、あなたらしくアセンションしていく準備が整ったのです。
思いきって扉を開けて、進んで行きましょう！

プロフィール

牧季

まき◎自動書記ナビゲーター。2013年よりアーティストとして活動を開始。アートを通して徐々に開き出したサイキック能力を使い、自動書記で描き下ろした作品は、スイス・ジュネーブにある国連欧州本部で開催された国際平和美術展にて展示され、その後、スペイン、オーストリア、アラブ首長国連邦、チェコ共和国などの美術展に出展。2018年に、自動書記でつながっていた先が、地球と人類のアセンションをサポートする宇宙連合だとわかり、彼らと共同で「STARSEED OF LIFE」を創始。同時期に日本神界ともつながり、自動書記で降ろす絵や文字、神音霊を用いたご神事も全国で行なう。現在は、覚醒を促す宇宙ぬり絵の普及や神社ツアー、リトリートなど開催している。2023年、東久邇宮文化褒賞受賞。
https://lit.link/starseedoflife

moved by the current heading towards Mt. Haleakala on the island of Maui, and we were astonished by the sight we saw there. The tour started in the evening, and after clearing the mind and body in the forests of Mt. Haleakala, we took a short break in the car while watching the sun set behind a sea of clouds.

Then, as the sky turned dark, I was lying on the empty ground and looking up at the sky. Surprisingly, there were glimpses of UFOs in the sky. I had never been able to see them properly, but on this day they appeared one after another.

Oh my Gosh! There were red and green lights passing through, some moving like fireflies, some drawing circles, some forming triangles, and before I knew it, there were 30 to 50 spaceships...I couldn't even count them anymore...they came flying, and there was a storm of joy!! It looked to me as if the UFOs were having a blast, dancing with joy.

Of course, it wasn't just me, my two friends who were with me also saw them.
I felt that the day when everyone can easily contact cosmic beings in this way is almost upon us. And I felt like they were telling me this:"Let's work together to contribute to the Earth."I felt with all my being that this is what the world would be like after Ascension.
Don't you think it would be as fun as a dream to be able to interact with cosmic beings like friends? The 7 Awakening Programs in "Cosmic Sutra Tracing" are tools for awakening that can give you a little chance, help, and support in order to live in such a world.

Having experienced this, you are now ready to ascend in your own way.
Let's open the doors and move forward!

Maki

Automatic writing navigator. She started her career as an artist in 2013. The work, which was drawn using automatic writing using the psychic abilities that were gradually developed through art, was exhibited at the International Peace Art Exhibition held at the United Nations European Headquarters in Geneva, Switzerland, and was subsequently exhibited in Spain, Austria, the United Arab Emirates and the Czech Republic, etc. In 2018, having discovered that the party she was connected to through automatic writing was the Space Federation, which supports the ascension of Earth and humanity, together they founded ``STARSEED OF LIFE.'' Around the same time, she became connected to the world of Japanese divinity, and has performed rituals all over the country using images and letters drawn using automatic writing, as well as divine sound spirits. Currently, she promotes cosmic coloring books that encourage awakening, and holding shrine tours and retreats. In 2023, she was awarded the Higashi-kuninomiya Culture Award.
https://lit.link/starseedoflife

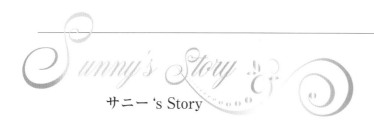

サニー 's Story

目に見えない存在たちと日常的に会話する

　Sunnyです。今回、縁あって、この宇宙写経の鑑定や、サポート存在からのチャネリングメッセージを担当することになったわけですが、私自身のことを少しお話ししますね。

　私は生まれつき、自然界の３次元の領域では見えない、聞こえないはずの天使や妖精、動植物と会話をすることができました。

　たとえば、幼い頃、なかなか寝付けないでいたとき、私の枕元に天使が現れ、海の底に眠るレムリアの輝かしい世界や、そこに住むユニコーンたちのことを話してくれて、それを子守歌のように心地よく聞きながら眠ることがよくありました。

　またあるとき、公園のブランコに乗り一人で揺られていると、傍にいた野良猫が、「僕たちは一人ぼっちが好きだと誤解されるけれど、いつでも友だちが欲しいと思っているんだ」と話しかけてくることもありました。私にとっては普通のそのことが、どうやら他の人にとっては異質で不可思議なことであると気がついてからは、変わり者扱いされることを怖れて、自分の力を周囲の人

に悟られないよう、細心の注意を払って隠していました。

　しかし、2012年頃から徐々に始まっていたアセンションの流れの中、そうした力は大切なギフトであり、役割なのだと、自分自身がサイキックであることを受け入れることができました。すると、時空や次元を超えて、それまでには会ったことのない天使やアセンテッドマスター、宇宙種族の存在たちとつながり、その意志をチャネリングする、ということが始まったのです。

　以来、さまざまな存在と日常的に会話するようになりました。高次元からの情報をビジョンや言葉、イメージでごく自然に受け取って、必要な方々にお届けするということをお仕事にするようにもなりました。そして、アネモネさんでも時折、異次元フォトや宇宙文字、過去世のストーリー、異次元から物質化した物の鑑定などを依頼され、皆さまにお伝えしています。

アシュタールの「スターシードミーティング」で隣りどうしだった

　牧季ちゃんと初めて出会ったのは、都内の喫茶店でした。　飾らない笑顔で佇む牧季ちゃんを見て、宇宙時代、アシュタールの声掛けにより集まったスターシードミー

Having Daily Conversations with Invisible Beings

This is Sunny. I am very pleased to be in charge of the interpretation of this cosmic sutra and the channeling messages from the supportive beings, but I would like to tell you a little about myself.

I was born with the ability to communicate with angels and fairies who cannot be seen or heard in the 3D realm of nature, as well as plants and animals.

For example, when I was a child and had trouble falling asleep, an angel appeared by my bedside and told me about the glorious world of Lemuria, which rests at the bottom of the ocean, and the unicorns that live there. I often fell asleep comfortably while listening to it.

Another time, when I was on a swing alone in a park, a stray cat nearby would sometimes come and say to me, "People misunderstand that we like to be alone, but we are always wanting friends."

After I realized that what was normal to me was somehow foreign and mysterious to other people, I began to fear being treated as an outcast and tried not to let the people around me realize my abilities, and hid them with great care.

However, during the Ascension process that had gradually begun around 2012, I was able to accept that I am a psychic, and that this power is an important gift and role. Then, I began to connect with angels, ascended masters, and cosmic race beings that I had never met before, and began to channel their will beyond time, space, and dimensions.

Since then, I have started having conversations with various beings on a daily basis. I made it my job to receive information naturally from higher dimensions through visions, words, and images, and deliver it to those who need them.

ティングで、隣りの席に座っていた大切な仲間だったことがわかりました。

そして、初めて「宇宙絵文字」を見たとき、紙面から発せられる青白い光やエネルギーの強さから、とにかく「すごいものを見てしまった！」という驚きと期待でいっぱいに。さらに、その意味をリーディングすると、膨大な情報量が詰まった宇宙からの絵巻物であることがわかり、とても興奮しました。

以前、アネモネ誌上で牧季ちゃんの自動書記を鑑定したときよりも格段に進化していて、しかも現物を目の当たりにし、次の瞬間、「自動書記や宇宙写経を私もやってみたい！」という衝動にかられたのです。

行くのではなく、その場に創り上げる35次元

私自身、サイキックチャネラーであるものの、自動書記や写経に対しては「その道の専門家にお任せしておけばよい、私ごときが下手に手を出すようなことではない」と思っていたので、これまでは一度もやってみたいという発想が湧かなかったのですが、牧季ちゃんから
「宇宙写経、やってみませんか？」
と言われたとき、

「わあ！いいんですか？」
と大喜びしている自分がいて、カラー筆ペンをその場で借りて、すぐにトライしてみました。すると、どうでしょう。
「えっ！手が勝手に動く！」
「塗り分けたい筆の色も、書き足したい言葉も、初めから私は知っている！」

呆然とする私の思考を置き去りに、勝手に動き出す手を眺めていると、だんだんと無我の意識に変化し、心地よい浮遊感に身を任せていると、急にすっと手が止まり、同時にこの写経は、目の前の牧季ちゃんへのプレゼントだということがわかりました。そして牧季ちゃん自身もそのことを理解し、おたがいに描いた写経を交換したのです。

そして、牧季ちゃんから
「いま浮かぶ数字は何？」
と問われ、私の唇を通じて出てきた数は、「35」でした。

これは、二人が写経を行ったことにより、周囲の世界から完全に分けられた異次元の領域を知るように牧季ちゃんが導き、出てきた答えです。そう、私たちはその場で「35次元」を体験していたのです。

anemone occasionally requests my interpretation of the photos, cosmic letters, past life stories, and materialized objects from other dimensions, and we have shared them with the readers.

We Were Next to Each Other at Ashtar's "Starseed Meeting"

The first time I met Maki-chan was at a coffee shop in Tokyo. When I saw Maki-chan standing there with a natural smile, I realized that she was a dear friend of mine who was sitting next to me at the Starseed Meeting that Ashtar called out to during the Cosmic days.

And when I saw the "Cosmic symbols" for the first time, I was filled with surprise and anticipation because of the blue-white light and the strength of the energy emitted from the paper, and I thought, "I have just seen something amazing!" Furthermore, when I read its meaning, I found out that it was a picture scroll from outer space filled with a huge amount of information, which made me very excited.

It had evolved dramatically since when I interpreted Maki-chan's automatic writing in *anemone* magazine, and when I saw it in person, the next moment I felt an urge to try automatic writing and Cosmic Sutra Tracing myself!

Creating the 35th Dimension on the Spot Instead of Going There

Although I am a psychic channeler myself, I had thought that automatic writing and tracing of sutras should be left to the experts in that field; it was not something someone like me could mess around with. So up until now, I never had the idea to try it, but when Maki-chan said to me "Wouldn't you like to try Cosmic Sutra Tracing?"

I was so excited that I replied, "Wow! Are you sure?" and borrowed a color brush pen on the spot and tried it out right away. And lo and

それは、歓喜そのものであり、ありのままの自分でいること、生きていることを祝福されている感覚、光そのものの世界でした。

いままでもチャネリングにより、高次元の世界には何度も行き来していましたが、それはあくまでもこちらから向かう領域、旅先でした。でも、このときに感じた35次元は、"自分たちがこの場に創り出した高次元"だったのです。

魂のシフト旅を経て、再びメッセージを降ろせるように

その後、この宇宙写経の本を作る流れになり、私も牧季ちゃんとともに著者になるという、生まれて初めてのはこびとなりました。私は、いつものように、自宅でアロマを焚き、瞑想をしてメッセージを訊き始めました。ところが、まったく降りてきません。上からの返事はこうでした。

「いまのあなたでは、受け取りきれない。伝えられない。」
私は愕然としました。

「16種族の宇宙存在の皆さん、多くの方があなたたちの言葉を待っています。私は一刻も早く、それを届けたいのです。」

必死でそう説明しましたが、相変わらず高次元存在たちは口をつぐんだままです。メッセージを降ろせないなんて……ショックと焦りでパニックになりそうな私の心情とは無関係に、仕事で、日常とはかけ離れた場所に行く機会が訪れました。それも立て続けに、です。

最初に訪れたのは、沖縄の浜比嘉島です。その場所でツインレイの男神シルミチューと女神アマミチューに出会い、無我の永遠の愛を教わり、傷ついた女性性や男性性の静かな統合の儀式を受けました。

次に呼ばれたのは、出雲の国のアマテラスとスサノオのもと。そこで、神降しの洗礼を受け、私の中の宇宙（自神）に光を当てられました。

そして最後は、ある水との出会いでした。その水は、すでに他界した預言者が、宇宙の膨大な叡智を器に転写、凝縮させたというもので、器に注がれた水を飲むことで覚醒が進むように意図された水です。その水を飲むと、どこか遠くに感じていた魂の望みが確信に変わりました。そう、私の魂の望みは、宇宙と地球をつなぐこと。直近の望みは、この宇宙写経のためのメッセージを降ろすことです。

behold!

"What! My hands are moving on their own!"

From the beginning, I knew which brush colors and words I wanted to add!

As I watched my hands move on their own, leaving behind my dumbfounded thoughts, my consciousness gradually changed to one of selflessness, and as I surrendered to the pleasant floating sensation, my hands suddenly stopped, and at the same time I realized that this traced sutra was a gift for Maki-chan who was in front of me. And Maki-chan herself also understood this, and we exchanged the traced sutras we had drawn.

And when asked "What number comes to mind right now?" from Maki-chan, the number that came out of my mouth was "35."

This is the answer that came about when the two of us traced the sutras, led by Maki-chan, to learn about a different dimensional realm completely separated from the surrounding world. Yes, we were experiencing the 35th dimension right then and there.

It was joy itself, a feeling of being blessed to be who I am and being alive. A world of light itself. Up until now, I had traveled to higher dimensions many times through channeling, but those were just realms and destinations for me to travel to. However, the 35th dimension that I felt at that time was a higher dimension that we created in that place.

Being Able to Channel Messages Again, after a Soul Shifting Journey

After that, the process of creating this book of cosmic sutras began, and I became the author along with Maki-chan, which was my first experience in life. As usual, I started burning incense at my home, meditating, and asking for messages. However, I couldn't download anything at all.

The reply from above was this: "You are unable

こうした儀式を通じて、私自身のエゴがそぎ落とされ、確実に覚醒が進んでいきました。そして、この一連の旅から帰って再びチャネリングすると、いままで以上にパワフルなメッセージが降りてきたのでした。私自身の何段階もの魂のシフトを経て初めて、この宇宙絵文字に込められた、アセンションするための真理を受け取ることができ、こうして皆さんにお届けすることができるようになったのです。

この本は、宇宙の大いなる計画のもと、たくさんの奇跡をつないであなたに届けられたアセンションツールです。本を開くと、ページを追うごとに新たな気づきがあることでしょう。あなたのハートが開き、心からの安心感が生まれ、サイキックの感性が開いていく感覚。また、あなたがなぜ、この世界に生まれてきたのか、魂に深くに刻まれたミッションを思い出す瞬間もあるかもしれません。

ひとつひとつの発見が、あなたをときめかせ、夢中にさせていくに違いありません。光と喜びの中で始まるあなたの旅を、どうぞ心ゆくまで楽しんでくださいね。

to accept it right now. We cannot convey it."
I was stunned.
"To all the 16 races of cosmic beings, many are waiting for your words. I want to deliver them as soon as possible."

I desperately tried to explain, but the higher-dimensional beings remained silent.

"I can't believe that I am unable to download messages..."
Regardless of my feelings of shock and impatience and being on the verge of panic, an opportunity arose for me to go to places far removed from my daily life for work. And in quick successions, too.

The first place I visited was Hamahiga Island in Okinawa. There, I met the twin-ray god Shirumi-chu and goddess Amami-chu, who taught me about selfless and eternal love, and underwent a ceremony to quietly unify the wounded feminine and masculine sides.

Next, I was called to Amaterasu and Susanoo

プロフィール

Le Soleil＊Sunny

る　それいゆ　さにー◎スピリチュアルチャネラー＆ヒーラー・ツインソウルフロンティア。生まれつき、自然界の精霊や動・植・鉱物、高次のマスターや宇宙存在など、無生物も含めたあらゆる存在物と会話でき、透視からヒーリングまでオールマイティなサイキック能力を持つ。また、過去世が映画のストーリーのように詳細に見え、オーラの読み解きとともに魂の使命やツインレイ診断など、愛に基づくメッセージを届けている。ソウルメイト・サイキック能力開発講座、オラクルカードリーディング講座などを年間１０回以上開催。個人セッションは半年先まで予約が埋まる。ツインレイパートナーの Zia と YouTube を配信。月刊『アネモネ』にて「コズミック天気予報」連載中。
https://lit.link/LeSoleil

in the country of Izumo. There, I received a divine initiation of channeling and a light was shed on the Universe (God-self) within me.

And finally, there was an encounter with a certain type of water. The water is said to have had the vast wisdom of the Universe transferred and condensed into a vessel, by a prophet who has already passed away, and is intended to promote awakening by drinking the water poured into the vessel. When I drank that water, my soul's hope, which had felt somewhere far away, turned into certainty. Yes, my soul's desire is to connect the Universe and the Earth. My immediate hope is to channel the messages for this Cosmic Sutra Tracing.

Through these rituals, my own ego was removed and my awakening steadily progressed. And when I returned from these series of trips and channeled again, I received messages that were even more powerful than before. It was only after going through many stages of my own soul shift that I was able to receive the truth for Ascension contained in these cosmic symbols, and now I am able to share it with you.

This book is an Ascension tool brought to you by connecting many miracles under the great plan of the Universe. When you open the book, you will discover something new with each page. The feeling of your heart opening, feeling a sense of peace from the bottom of your heart, and a feeling of your psychic senses opening. There may also be moments when you remember why you were born into this world and the mission deeply engraved in your soul.

Each discovery is sure to thrill you and make you fall in love with it. Please enjoy your journey to the fullest as it begins in light and joy.

Le Soleil ＊ Sunny

Spiritual Channeler & Healer, Twin Soul Frontier. Born with the ability to communicate with all kinds of beings, including inanimate objects, such as spirits of the natural world, animals, plants, and minerals, higher dimensional masters, and cosmic beings, she possesses all-encompassing psychic abilities ranging from clairvoyance to healing. Additionally, she is able to see past lives in detail like a movie, and along with deciphering auras, she delivers messages based on love such as soul missions and twin ray assessment. She holds soulmate psychic ability development courses, oracle card reading courses, etc. more than 10 times a year. Private sessions are booked up to six months in advance. Together with her twin flame partner Zia , they stream on YouTube. "Cosmic Weather Forecast" is currently being serialized in the monthly magazine "*anemone*".
https://lit.link/LeSoleil

この本の二人の宇宙プロデューサーより

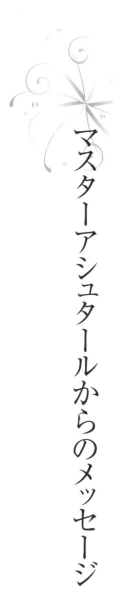

Message from Master Ashtar

私はアシュタール。
銀河の真理と調和を守る宙（そら）の旅人。
スターシードの民よ。私を覚えていますか？
かつてあなたたちは、私の呼び声に応え、
地球と人類のアセンションを牽引することを自ら志願しました。
そして、2万6000年に一度の祝祭のタイミングを見はからい、
目醒めることを決めて地球にジャンプした星の欠片（かけら）です。
地球に降り立った後のあなたたちの健気なチャレンジを、
私も宇宙の創造主もずっと見ていました。
その尊い努力は決して無駄ではありません。
なぜなら、その経験が、あなたたちをより強く成長させたからです。
あなたたちのミッションは、新生地球に自らの楽園を創ること。
その肉体を使い、魂のビジョンを実現していくことです。
一人ひとりが独自の個性を発揮して、
光のインフルエンサーとなってください。
あなたたちが光の旗印を立て、多くの者の希望となるのです。
忘れないでください。
私はいつもあなた達を見守っています。

I am Ashtar.

I am a traveler in the Universe who protects the truth and harmony of the galaxy. Starseed people, do you remember me?

You once answered my call, and volunteered to lead the ascension of Earth and humanity.

And, judging the timing to be right for the festival, which happens once every 26,000 years, you are the star fragments that decided to awaken and jump over to Earth.

Both I and the Creator of the Universe have been watching your admirable challenges after your descending on Earth.

Your precious efforts will never be in vain.

Because that experience has made you grow stronger.

Your mission is to create your own paradise on the new Earth.

It is about using the body to realize the vision of the soul.

May each of you exhibit your own individuality and become an influencer of light.

You will hoist a banner of light and become the hope for many.

Please do not forget.

I am always watching over you.

From the Two Cosmic Producers of this Book

Message from Master Hilarion

私はヒラリオン。
第五光線を使い、科学やテクノロジー、
スピリチュアルの知識と叡智を司る光の使者です。
アセンションし、霊的存在に変容していくあなたたちの
ファシリテーターとして現れました。
今、目まぐるしい上昇気流の渦の中、
あなたたちの精神や肉体は、急ピッチで変化しています。
そのため、原因不明の身体の不調や、
心が掻き乱されるような出来事に苦痛を感じている人も
いることでしょう。
しかし、心配には及びません。
それらはすべて、ライトボディにシフトするための一時的な不調和です。
クリーンな水を飲み、新鮮な野菜や果物を中心に食べ、
太陽のサイクルに合わせた早寝早起きを心掛けます。
また、ライトボディとは共鳴しない曇りや迷い、
疑念や執着は、浮上するたびに丁寧に手放します。
歓喜の旗を翻し、新しい待ちわびた世界の扉を開くのです。

I am Hilarion.

I am the messenger of light who, using the fifth ray, governs science and technology, spiritual knowledge and wisdom.

I have appeared as a facilitator to those of you who are ascending and transforming into spiritual beings.

Now, in the midst of a dizzying updraft, your mind and body are changing at a rapid pace.

As a result, I am sure there are some people who are feeling pain due to physical problems of unknown cause, or upsetting events.

But do not worry.

They are all temporary disharmony in order to shift into the light body.

Drink clean water, eat mainly fresh vegetables and fruits, try to go to bed early and wake up early to match the sun's cycle.

Also, carefully let go of cloudiness and hesitation, doubts and attachments that do not resonate with the light body, as they arise.

Wave the flag of joy and open the door to a long awaited new world.

マスターヒラリオンからのメッセージ

宇宙写経

Cosmic Sutra Tracing

2024 年 5 月 28 日　初版発行

著者　　　　牧季／ Le Soleil＊Sunny
訳者　　　　ウォーカー由里子
編集　　　　中田真理亜
デザイン　　西尾好恵
イラスト　　藤井由美子
翻訳協力　　ローレン・ウィルキー
発行者　　　奥山竜紀
プロデュース　宇宙連合の皆さん
発行所　　　株式会社ルドラクシャ
　　　　　　〒 165-0023 東京都中野区江原町 3-12-4
発売所　　　株式会社めるくまーる
　　　　　　〒 101-0051 東京都千代田区神田神保町 1 -11
　　　　　　信ビルディング 4 F
　　　　　　TEL03-3518-2003 FAX03-3518-2004
印刷所　　　株式会社シナノ

First edition issued　May 28, 2024

Author　　　　Maki ／ Le Soleil＊Sunny

Translator　　Yuriko Walker

Editor　　　　Maria Nakada

Design　　　　Yoshie Nishio

Illustrator　　Yumiko Fujii

Translation Assistance

　　　　　　　Lauren Wilke

Issuer　　　　Tatsunori Okuyama

Produce　　　Members of the Space Federation

Publisher　　Rudraksha Corp.

　　　　　　　3-12-4 Ehara-cho, Nakano-ku, Tokyo, 1650023

　　　　　　　Japan

Sales Publisher

　　　　　　　Merkmal Corp.

　　　　　　　1-11 Shin building 4F Kanda-Jinbou-cho, Chiyoda-
　　　　　　　ku, Tokyo, 1010051 Japan

Printing　　　Shinano.,Ltd

ISBN978-4-8397-0187-1　C0076